THINKING LIKE A WINNER
A GUIDE TO HIGH PERFORMANCE LEADERSHIP

by

Mark J. Martinko, Ph.D.

Gulf Coast Publishing, LLC
Tallahassee, Florida

Copyright © 2002 Gulf Coast Publishing, LLC.

All rights reserved. No part of this publication may be reproduced, stored on a retrieval system, or transmitted, in any form or by any means, electronic, mechanical, photocopying, microfilming, recording or otherwise, without written permission from the publisher.

ISBN: 0-9717525-0-8 (paper)
0-9717525-1-6 (cloth)
Library of Congress Number: 2002102480

Printed in the United States of America

Contact Gulf Coast Publishing, LLC: 850-893-2786 (Voice); 850-893-1093 (Fax); E-mail: martinko@netally.com

CONTENTS

	PREFACE	vii
	ACKNOWLEDGMENTS	ix
	TO THE READER	xi
CHAPTER I	**INTRODUCTION**	**1**
CHAPTER II	**SELF-ASSESSMENT**	**5**
	Part I	5
	Part II	10
CHAPTER III	**CAUSAL REASONING**	**17**
	Attribution Styles and Dimensions	18
	Potential Attribution Styles	21
CHAPTER IV	**THE ARCHETYPAL OPTIMIST**	**24**
CHAPTER V	**THE PESSIMISTIC CR STYLE**	**28**
CHAPTER VI	**INTERPRETING THE SELF-TEST: PART I**	**32**
	LOC Scores	33
	LOC Scores for Success Events	33
	LOC Scores for Failure Events	34
	Stability Scores	35
	Stability Scores for Success Events	36
	Stability Score for Failure Events	36
	Overall Assessment	37
CHAPTER VII	**THE SIXTEEN CAUSAL REASONING TYPES**	**39**
	Mr. or Ms. Responsible	39
	The Doer	42
	Mr. or Ms. Wonderful	42
	The Optimist	43
	The Martyr	43
	The Self-Made Man/Woman	43
	The Politician	44
	The Victim	44
	The Accommodator	45

	The Plugger	45
	The Blamer	45
	The Hippie	46
	The Pessimist	46
	Mr. or Ms. Tragic	47
	The Dependent	47
	The Socialite	48
	Conclusion	48
CHAPTER VIII	**THE EMOTIONALLY INTELLIGENT CAUSAL REASONING STYLE: BOBBY BOWDEN AND NUMBER 11**	**49**
	Coach Bowden	50
	The National Championship Victory	51
	The Defeat at the Orange Bowl to Oklahoma	53
	Florida State Loss to the University of Florida—1983	54
	West Virginia's Loss to Pitt at Pitt	55
	Beating Michigan at Michigan—1991	56
	Pitt at West Virginia	57
	Number 11	60
	The 1995 Regional Tournament and College World Series	60
	The 1992 Club	62
	Barry Blackwell	63
	The 1993 Season	64
	The 1995 Club	66
	Philosophy	66
	Luck and Chance	67
	Faith	68
	Concluding Comments	69
CHAPTER IX	**PERCEPTUAL BIASES THAT CLOUD CAUSAL REASONING**	**71**
	The Self-Serving Bias	72
	The Actor-Observer Bias	73
	False Consensus Effect	75
	Hedonic Relevance	76
	The Effect of CR Biases on Interpersonal Relations	76
	The Effect of CR Biases on the Self and Self-Motivation	80
CHAPTER X	**TOWARD AN EMOTIONALLY INTELLIGENT CR STYLE: OVERCOMING THE EFFECTS OF CR BIASES**	**83**
	Removing Ambiguity	83
	Hedonic Relevance	85
	Developing Empathy	87
	Increasing Physical Proximity and Interaction	88
	Impression Management	89
	Multiple Raters	90
	Attributional Retraining	90
	Structured Experiences for Groups and Organizations	100
	Concluding Comments	101

Contents

CHAPTER XI	**INTERPRETING THE SELF-TEST: PART II**	**104**
	LOC Scores	106
	LOC Scores for Success Events	106
	LOC Scores for Failure Events	107
	Stability Scores	108
	Stability Score for Success Events	109
	Stability Score for Failure Events	109
	Overall Assessment	110
CHAPTER XII	**THE SIXTEEN SOCIAL CR STYLES**	**112**
	The Horse Trainer	113
	The Split Personality	113
	The Empathizer	116
	The Optimist	116
	The Discreditor I	117
	The Slave Driver	117
	Mr. or Ms. Arrogant	118
	The Cheerleader	118
	The Faultfinder	119
	The Blamer	119
	The Environmentalist	119
	Mr. or Ms. Gravytrain	120
	The Pessimist	120
	Mr. or Ms. Abusive	121
	Mr. or Ms. Inconsequential	121
	The Discreditor II	122
CHAPTER XIII	**MANAGING INTERPERSONAL CR STYLES**	**123**
	Ignoring The Bias	125
	Leveling	126
	Diagnosing the Bias and Providing Helpful Feedback	127
	Objective Third Parties	127
	Managing Helplessness	128
	Immunization	129
	Discrimination Training	129
	Perceptions of Rewards	130
	Modeling	130
	Ego Defense	131
	Attribution Counseling	131
	Organizationally-Induced Helplessness	132
CHAPTER XIV	**THE BIG PICTURE**	**136**
	Toward a Model of Optimal Performance	136
	The Environment	137
	The Individual	137
	Causal Reasoning	139
	Expectancies	141
	Goal Setting	142
	Behaviors	143
	Outcomes	144
	Challenges in the Application of the Model	146

CHAPTER XV	**HOT TOPICS AND APPLICATIONS**	**150**
	Empowerment	150
	Elite Performance	151
	Dysfunctional Behavior	153
	Self-Esteem and Self-Efficacy	156
	Impression Management	157
	Emotional Intelligence	158
	Cross-Cultural Management	162
	Performance Appraisals	162
	Selection Processes	163
	Charismatic and Transformational Leadership	164
	Final Thoughts	164
	NOTES AND REFERENCES	**168**
	ABOUT THE AUTHOR	**177**

PREFACE

Today it seems like every popular book about leadership and motivation has a list of ten steps to success. If we examine these lists, we find that there are often vast differences in the factors that are included. It doesn't take a rocket scientist to figure out that they can't all be right. Nevertheless, authors continue to sell popular books based on oversimplified assumptions about the factors that generate personal and organizational success.

This book is an attempt to go beyond these simplistic formulas and give a more realistic description of at least some of the factors that are critical for achieving optimal individual and organizational performance. It is an attempt to talk to rather than down to the reader. It assumes that the reader is willing to explore complicated relationships if they are explained clearly and are free of the academic jargon that so often clouds our ability and motivation to learn new concepts.

The need to write this book was motivated by several sources. When I first started to train managers at Western Electric, the head of the Engineering Department insisted that there must be some formula that could be translated into a questionnaire capable of identifying job candidates who would be outstanding performers. I told him that I was not aware of any such formula. I have been trying to develop a more credible answer ever since. A second major influence was a study of high performing school principals that I was commissioned to do by the Department of Education of the State of Florida. As a part of that grant, our research team interviewed and observed forty-one school principals for 270 days, recording 15,000 pages of minute-by-minute descriptions of the principals' behaviors. Each of the more than 40,000 events was then coded and analyzed to identify the differences between the high and average performers. Our study served as a major building block for the foundation for the Florida Department of Education's competency-based system for selecting, training, evaluating, rewarding, and retaining high performing school leaders. The insights gained from that experience have greatly influenced my thinking and motivation to unravel the intricacies of high performance.

Perhaps the most important influence on my motivation to write this book is the research that I have read and conducted over the past 25 years that focuses on the ways in which successful versus unsuccessful people think. At this point I am absolutely convinced that, although a person's objective reality and personal characteristics obviously create opportunities and obstacles, it is the way people think about their successes and failures that is the primary factor differentiating those individuals who consistently succeed versus those who frequently fail. In this book, we will explore the areas of cognitive psychology which deal with causal reasoning (i.e., how people think about their successes and failures) and show how these thought processes are major factors in the emotional intelligence that enables empowerment or helplessness for both one's self and others.

ACKNOWLEDGMENTS

Throughout my career, I have been blessed by great mentors. Peg Clifford at the University of Iowa gave me the encouragement I needed to pursue an academic career. Ken Fielding at Omaha Public Power District both challenged me and demonstrated confidence in me, which was much needed when, as a twenty-five-year-old, I taught basic supervision to a group of supervisors who had an average of 15 years experience.

Fred Luthans, my advisor at the University of Nebraska, has been instrumental throughout my career by encouraging me to pursue a doctorate in business, offering numerous publishing and consulting opportunities, and by his friendship.

I have been privileged to work with and mentor a great group of doctoral students including Bill Gardner (University of Mississippi), Russell Kent and Constance Campbell (Georgia Southern University), Sherry Moss (Florida International University), Neal Thomson (Columbus State University), Scott Douglas (University of Montana), and Michael Gundlach who is finishing his degree at Florida State. The questions and issues that we have addressed as a group have contributed significantly to the development of the concepts that appear in this book.

Considerable gratitude also goes to the research community. An annotated set of references that acknowledge specific contributions for each chapter is provided at the end of the book. However, particular thanks go to Bernard

Weiner and Martin Seligman whose works have been particularly influential.

Florida State University has also been instrumental in my development. In particular I have appreciated the support of my dean, Melvin Stith, as well as coaches Bobby Bowden and Mike Martin who were interviewed for this book.

Finally, thanks go to the many practicing managers and students who contributed to and challenged my thoughts as participants in management seminars as well as in undergraduate and graduate classes. The many jobs and bosses that I have had in the past at McDonald's, U.S. Steel, Sheller-Globe Corporation, Western Electric, and Gulf Oil have provided a rich base of personal experience demonstrating both appropriate and inappropriate behaviors. In addition, the many small business owners that I have established friendships with in the Tallahassee area have also made significant contributions.

TO THE READER

I hope you like this book and find the information to be helpful. My intent in writing the book is to provide a practical and useful summary of the recent work in the area of motivation and leadership. I consider this book to be a work in progress and encourage you to provide any feedback that you may have that could improve the book. You can provide written feedback via email (martinko@nettally.com) or by conventional mail addressed to me at Gulf Coast Publishing, 3779 Forsythe Way, Tallahassee, FL 32308. I look forward to hearing from you.

At the end of the book is a section entitled notes and references. This section is provided to help inquisitive readers as well as my academic colleagues explore more fully the foundations of the material described in the various chapters.

DEDICATION

I had several people and groups in mind while writing this book. First, it is dedicated to everyone who has had to work for a crummy boss and all of those bosses who have had to manage uncooperative and poorly performing people. I hope this book provides some light for both groups. It is also dedicated to those rare and wonderful bosses, co-workers, and employees who have modeled the emotional intelligence described in this book. They have been the real teachers and we owe them a great debt of gratitude. Finally, 5% of my net proceeds from this book will go to the Fellowship for Christian Athletes, an organization that is close to the hearts of coaches Bobby Bowden and Mike Martin, who graciously agreed to be interviewed for this book.

CHAPTER 1

INTRODUCTION

At the 1996 Masters at Augusta, Greg Norman was far ahead of the field after three rounds of impeccable golf. On the final day, he failed to keep his six-stroke lead, losing to Nick Faldo. Although more than a hundred and fifty other golfers also "lost" the tournament, reporters descended on Norman like a flock of vultures. During the press conference that followed, Norman remained calm. He said that the sun would shine tomorrow and that he would be the same person tomorrow that he was today. He concluded by saying everybody's game has ups and downs, that golf had been very good to him, and that it would continue to be good for him.

In 1993 the Buffalo Bills lost their third consecutive Super Bowl. During the game, their star running back Thurman Thomas fumbled the ball three times. As in Norman's case, the media descended on Thomas and pointedly asked him if he felt responsible for the loss. Thomas's answer was similar to the bumper sticker "S_it happens." He quietly and politely explained that any time a running back carries a ball more than thirty times in a game, "things happen." Thus, Thurman Thomas, like Greg Norman, neither totally accepted or denied responsibility for the defeat.

The 1998 Super Bowl victory by the Denver Broncos was also followed by a series of interesting interviews. After the game, John Elway, who had "failed" three times before, admitted he had not played his best game. He credited his teammates, particularly Terrell Davis, his own parents, and his family for the victory. Terrell Davis gave credit to his offensive line, John Elway, his doctor who had administered a shot that relieved him of his migraine, and God. On the other hand, Brett Favre explained the loss of the Green Bay Packers by acknowledging that the Broncos had played an exceptional game and that his team simply ran out of time.

In the last few years, Tiger Woods has compiled a record in professional golf that is already legendary. In a recent article in *Sports Illustrated*, S.L. Price noted that when Tiger turned pro he said, "I expect to win every time." At first, many of the players felt that the statement was boastful. But before long, many of the top pros like Tom Lehman saw that he really believed it, and that he was winning at an unprecedented rate. Now the old pros are changing their mindsets, attempting to capture the same mindset as Tiger with the belief that the key to winning is believing in yourself. More recently, after breaking out of a slump and winning two tournaments, Tiger was asked how he would handle a "defeat" at the 2001 Masters. Surprisingly, his answer was similar to Greg Norman's back in 1996. He basically said that the sun would rise on Monday morning after the Masters and that he would still be the same person regardless of whether he won or lost. Now Tiger is talking like the old pros, indicating that it is hard to win without a little luck and a few of the right bounces.

The basic premise of this book is that the way people think about their successes and failures is a key factor in empowering future successes and in setting up future failures. Most of us believe this premise. That is why our eyes are glued to the TV set to see how great athletes, politicians, corporate leaders, and celebrities handle their successes and failures. We all believe, at least implicitly, that people who achieve great successes have a formula for success that they can share with us. The good news is that, from the perspective of the theory and research that we will discuss, there is a specific pattern of beliefs that almost always accompanies great performances and successful people. The limitation, as we shall see, is that these belief patterns develop over years of experience and cannot be changed easily. Nevertheless, as will be demonstrated below, these patterns can be recognized and change is possible.

This book is intended to help anyone who is interested in achieving optimal performance as an individual or as a manager and team leader. The first part of the book explains how our thought patterns affect motivation from an individual perspective and provides suggestions regarding strategies for maximizing your own performance and empowering others to achieve at optimal levels. The second part of the book discusses how our motivational belief systems affect the way we interact with others. In the cases of both Greg Norman and Thurman Thomas, the reporters had their own beliefs as to why they had "failed." Similarly, the reporters had their own beliefs as to why John Elway and Tiger Woods succeeded. These beliefs about success and failure affected the questions the reporters asked and how they treated each of these athletes. In a similar fashion, the beliefs we have about others affect the way we interact with and treat others including co-workers, subordinates, and family members. What we say and how we act can have profound empowering effects on others. On the other hand, our actions and words can also be denigrating and destroy rather than build motivation in others. Thus, the second part of the book is concerned with how these belief systems work and how we can change them so that we are a source of empowerment for others as well as ourselves.

The final section of the book broadens the discussion of leadership and optimal performance. Unlike many authors who write books on leadership and empowerment, I do not believe that a simple list of ten principles will make you, me, or anyone else a high performer. Although causal reasoning is a key factor that cannot be ignored in explaining and empowering optimal performance, other factors also play a role in the larger context of leadership and empowerment such as goal setting and reinforcement. The last section will place causal reasoning within the context of other motivation and leadership theories with which you are already familiar.

Finally, throughout the book, examples from businesses, sports teams, and other venues are used to illustrate points. I particularly like the examples from sports because a high percentage of readers will be familiar with the situations and thus will be able to relate to the examples. In addition, examples from sports are easy to use because athletes, teams, and athletic events have very clear sets of measurable objectives and goals. Unfortunately the goals of most Fortune 500 companies are not nearly as clear. The objectives of a manager in state government are often even less clear. Nevertheless, the basic elements of achievement-oriented motivation and leadership for both individuals and groups are similar regardless of whether the venue is an athletic or business event. Thus, even if the examples do not approximate your performance environment exactly, there is an implicit set of goals in all performance environments. The fact that you have your own goals should allow you to generalize from the examples used in the book to your specific performance environment. More discussion regarding the differences in performance environments and how they affect leadership and motivation will be provided in the last section of the book.

KEY POINTS

1. The way people think about their successes and failures is a key factor in empowering future successes and in setting up future failures.

2. There is a specific pattern of beliefs that almost always accompanies great performances and successful people.

3. Belief patterns develop over years of experience and cannot be changed easily.

4. These patterns can be recognized and change is possible.

5. The beliefs we have about others affect the way we interact with and treat others.

6. This book is intended to help anyone who is interested in achieving optimal performance as an individual or as a manager and team leader.

CHAPTER II

SELF-ASSESSMENT

Before beginning our discussion, it will be helpful to see how you think about your own successes and failures as well as the successes and failures of others. Listed below are some hypothetical situations. Try to place yourself in each of the situations, within your current job context, and answer the following questions.

PART I

1. Imagine that you have been just been told by your manager that you will not receive the promotion you have been hoping to receive.

   To what extent do you believe that each of the following factors would have contributed to you not receiving the promotion you desired?

   a. Lack of Ability

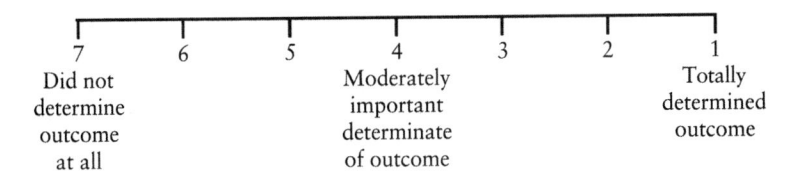

7	6	5	4	3	2	1
Did not determine outcome at all			Moderately important determinate of outcome			Totally determined outcome

b. Lack of Effort

```
┌───────┬───────┬───────┬───────┬───────┬───────┐
7       6       5       4       3       2       1
Did not                 Moderately              Totally
determine               important               determined
outcome                 determinate             outcome
at all                  of outcome
```

c. The Difficulty of getting promoted

```
┌───────┬───────┬───────┬───────┬───────┬───────┐
1       2       3       4       5       6       7
Did not                 Moderately              Totally
determine               important               determined
outcome                 determinate             outcome
at all                  of outcome
```

d. Bad Luck

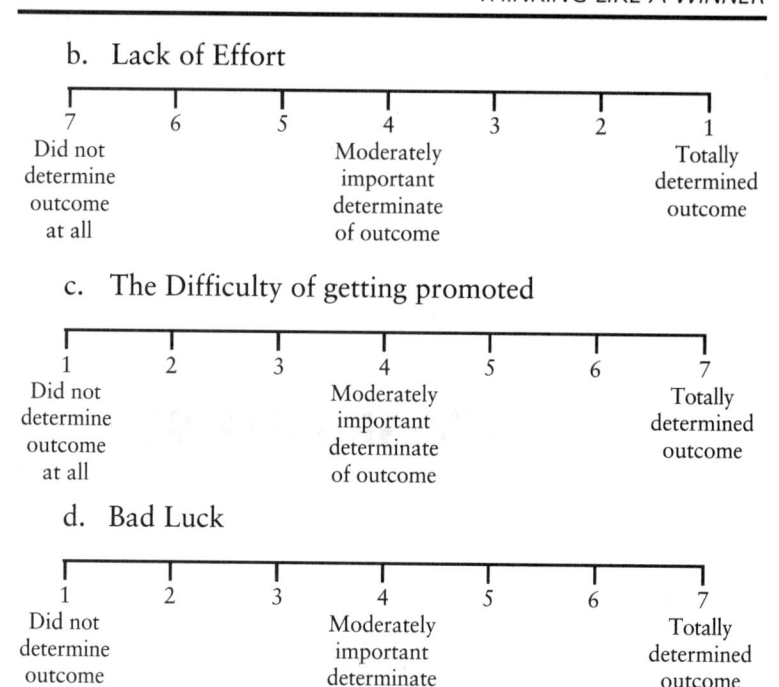

```
┌───────┬───────┬───────┬───────┬───────┬───────┐
1       2       3       4       5       6       7
Did not                 Moderately              Totally
determine               important               determined
outcome                 determinate             outcome
at all                  of outcome
```

e. To what extent are the reasons you did not receive the promotion due to things about you or due to other people or circumstances?

```
┌───────┬───────┬───────┬───────┬───────┬───────┐
1       2       3       4       5       6       7
Completely                              Completely due
due to me                                to other
                                         people or
                                         circumstances
```

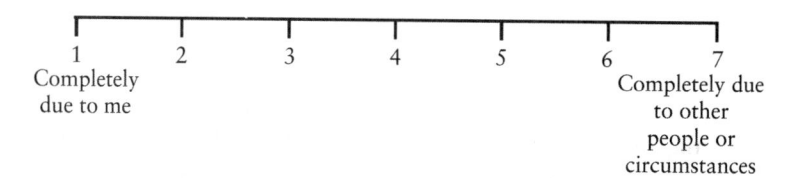

f. To what extent will the reasons you did not receive the promotion:

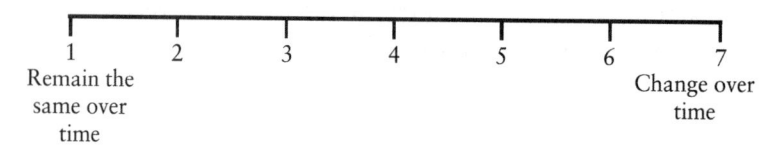

```
┌───────┬───────┬───────┬───────┬───────┬───────┐
1       2       3       4       5       6       7
Remain the                              Change over
same over                                time
time
```

2. Imagine that you have been just been told by your manager that you will not receive the raise you have been hoping to receive.

Self-Assessment

To what extent do you believe that each of the following factors would have contributed to you not receiving the raise you desired?

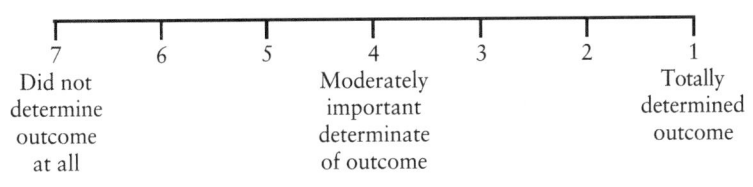

a. Lack of Ability

```
|————|————|————|————|————|————|
 7     6    5     4     3    2    1
Did not          Moderately        Totally
determine         important       determined
outcome         determinate        outcome
at all           of outcome
```

b. Lack of Effort

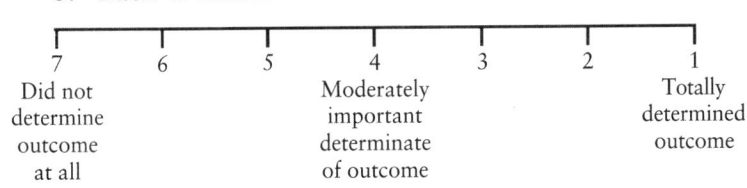

```
|————|————|————|————|————|————|
 7     6    5     4     3    2    1
Did not          Moderately        Totally
determine         important       determined
outcome         determinate        outcome
at all           of outcome
```

c. The Difficulty of getting a raise

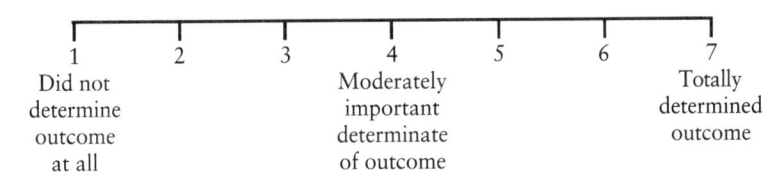

```
|————|————|————|————|————|————|
 1     2    3     4     5    6    7
Did not          Moderately        Totally
determine         important       determined
outcome         determinate        outcome
at all           of outcome
```

d. Bad Luck

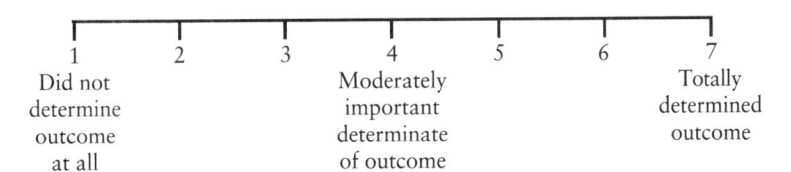

```
|————|————|————|————|————|————|
 1     2    3     4     5    6    7
Did not          Moderately        Totally
determine         important       determined
outcome         determinate        outcome
at all           of outcome
```

e. To what extent are the reasons you did not receive the raise due to things about you or due to other people or circumstances?

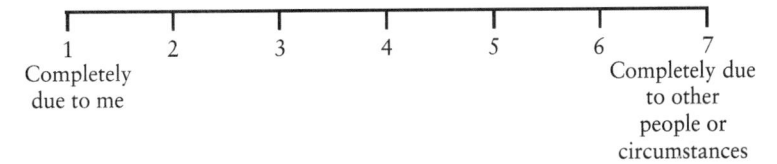

```
|————|————|————|————|————|————|
 1     2    3     4     5    6    7
Completely                      Completely due
due to me                         to other
                                 people or
                                circumstances
```

f. To what extent will the reasons you did not receive the raise:

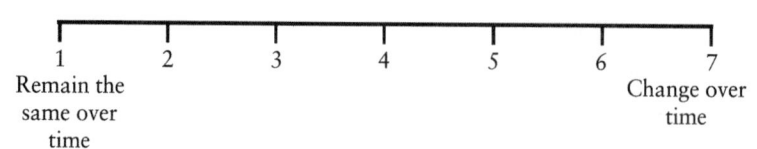

```
1     2     3     4     5     6     7
Remain the                      Change over
same over                          time
time
```

3. Imagine that you have been just been told by your manager that you will receive the promotion you have been hoping to receive.

   To what extent do you believe that each of the following factors would have contributed to your receiving the promotion you desired?

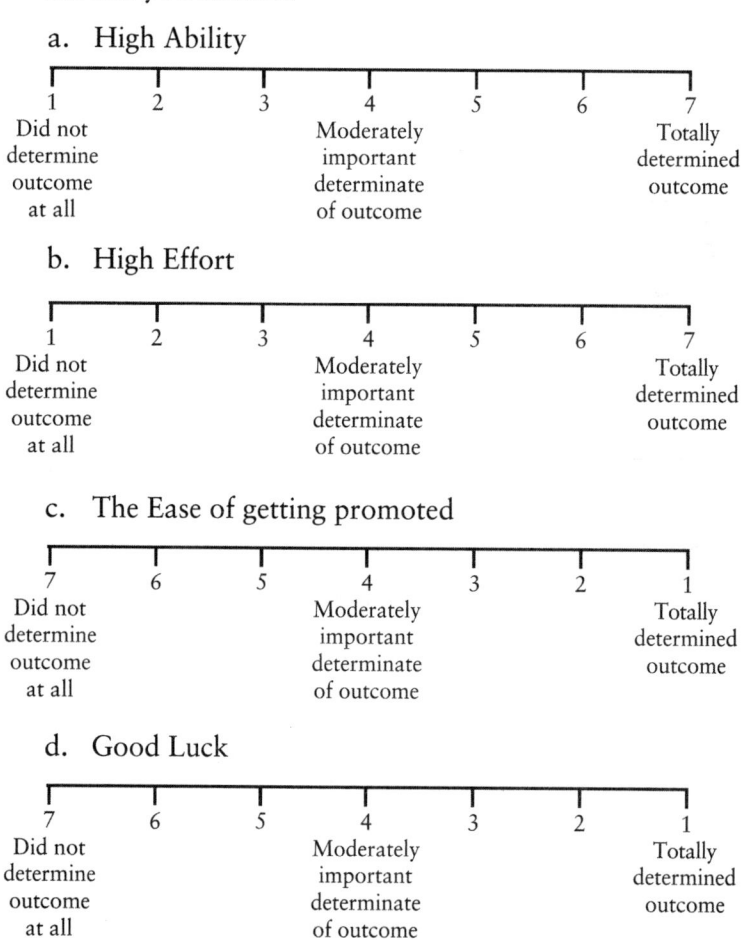

   a. High Ability

   ```
   1         2     3         4         5     6         7
   Did not               Moderately              Totally
   determine              important             determined
   outcome               determinate             outcome
   at all                of outcome
   ```

   b. High Effort

   ```
   1         2     3         4         5     6         7
   Did not               Moderately              Totally
   determine              important             determined
   outcome               determinate             outcome
   at all                of outcome
   ```

   c. The Ease of getting promoted

   ```
   7         6     5         4         3     2         1
   Did not               Moderately              Totally
   determine              important             determined
   outcome               determinate             outcome
   at all                of outcome
   ```

   d. Good Luck

   ```
   7         6     5         4         3     2         1
   Did not               Moderately              Totally
   determine              important             determined
   outcome               determinate             outcome
   at all                of outcome
   ```

e. To what extent are the reasons you received the promotion due to things about you or due to other people or circumstances?

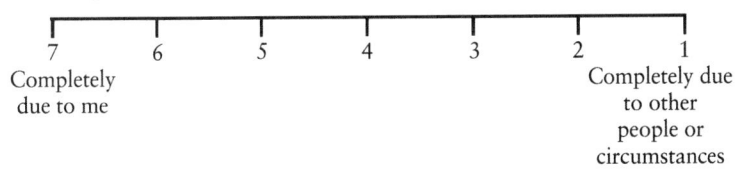

```
├──────┬──────┬──────┬──────┬──────┬──────┤
7      6      5      4      3      2      1
Completely                          Completely due
due to me                           to other
                                    people or
                                    circumstances
```

f. To what extent will the reasons you received the promotion:

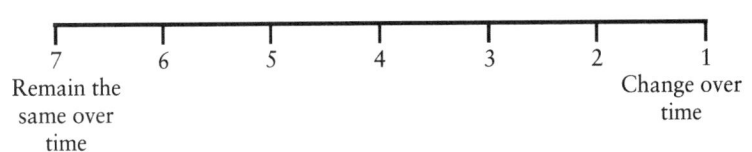

```
├──────┬──────┬──────┬──────┬──────┬──────┤
7      6      5      4      3      2      1
Remain the                          Change over
same over                           time
time
```

4. Imagine that you have been just been told by your manager that you will receive the raise you have been expecting.

   To what extent do you believe that each of the following factors would have contributed to your receiving the raise you have been expecting?

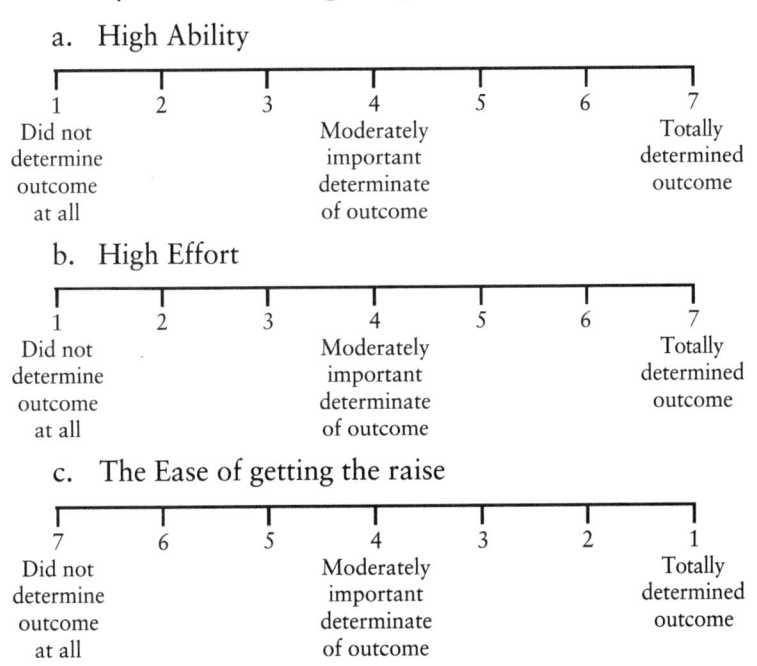

   a. High Ability

```
├──────┬──────┬──────┬──────┬──────┬──────┤
1      2      3      4      5      6      7
Did not               Moderately          Totally
determine             important           determined
outcome               determinate         outcome
at all                of outcome
```

   b. High Effort

```
├──────┬──────┬──────┬──────┬──────┬──────┤
1      2      3      4      5      6      7
Did not               Moderately          Totally
determine             important           determined
outcome               determinate         outcome
at all                of outcome
```

   c. The Ease of getting the raise

```
├──────┬──────┬──────┬──────┬──────┬──────┤
7      6      5      4      3      2      1
Did not               Moderately          Totally
determine             important           determined
outcome               determinate         outcome
at all                of outcome
```

d. Good Luck

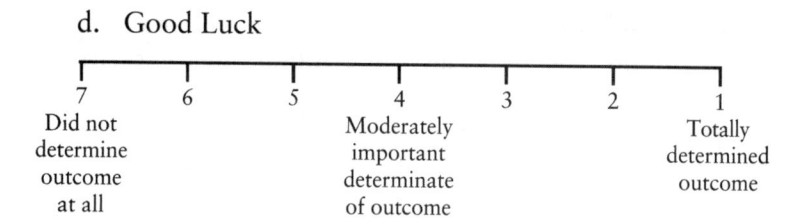

```
┌───────┬───────┬───────┬───────┬───────┬───────┬───────┐
7       6       5       4       3       2       1
Did not                 Moderately                      Totally
determine               important                       determined
outcome                 determinate                     outcome
at all                  of outcome
```

e. To what extent are the reasons you received the raise due to things about you or due to other people or circumstances?

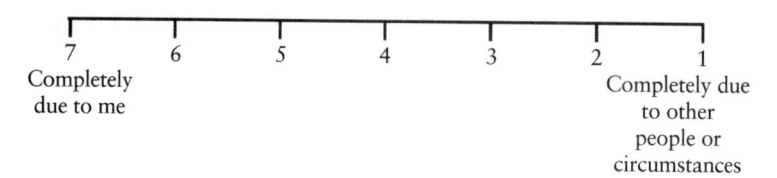

```
┌───────┬───────┬───────┬───────┬───────┬───────┬───────┐
7       6       5       4       3       2       1
Completely                                      Completely due
due to me                                       to other
                                                people or
                                                circumstances
```

f. To what extent will the reasons you received the raise:

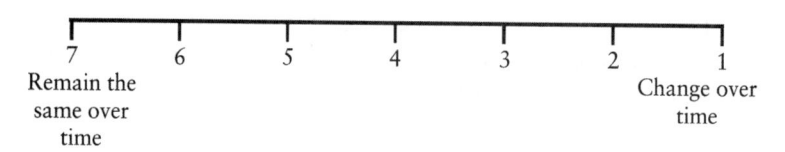

```
┌───────┬───────┬───────┬───────┬───────┬───────┬───────┐
7       6       5       4       3       2       1
Remain the                                      Change over
same over                                       time
time
```

PART II

Listed below are some additional hypothetical situations similar to the ones above. However, these situations are concerned with the successes and failures of others. Try to imagine the typical person you work with and imagine these situations happening to your typical co-worker. Then answer the questions that follow.

1. Imagine that you have just heard that one of your typical co-workers will not receive the promotion that the co-worker was hoping to receive.

   To what extent do you believe that each of the following factors would have contributed to the co-worker not receiving the desired promotion?

a. Lack of Ability

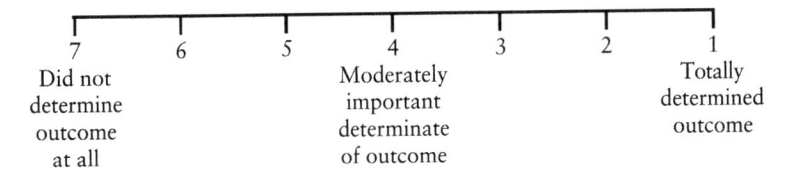

```
┌───┬───┬───┬───┬───┬───┐
7   6   5   4   3   2   1
Did not         Moderately      Totally
determine       important       determined
outcome         determinate     outcome
at all          of outcome
```

b. Lack of Effort

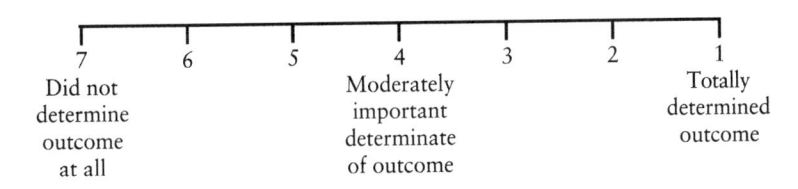

```
┌───┬───┬───┬───┬───┬───┐
7   6   5   4   3   2   1
Did not         Moderately      Totally
determine       important       determined
outcome         determinate     outcome
at all          of outcome
```

c. The Difficulty of getting a promotion

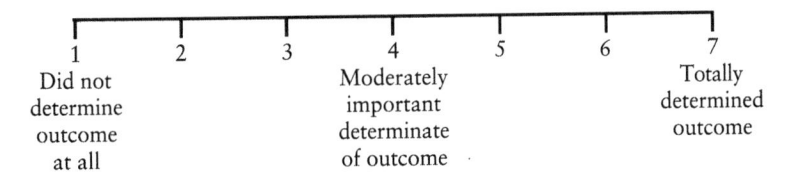

```
┌───┬───┬───┬───┬───┬───┐
1   2   3   4   5   6   7
Did not         Moderately      Totally
determine       important       determined
outcome         determinate     outcome
at all          of outcome
```

d. Bad Luck

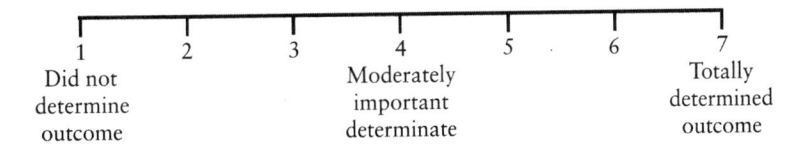

```
┌───┬───┬───┬───┬───┬───┐
1   2   3   4   5   6   7
Did not         Moderately      Totally
determine       important       determined
outcome         determinate     outcome
```

e. To what extent are the reasons the co-worker did not receive the promotion due to something about the co-worker or due to other people or circumstances?

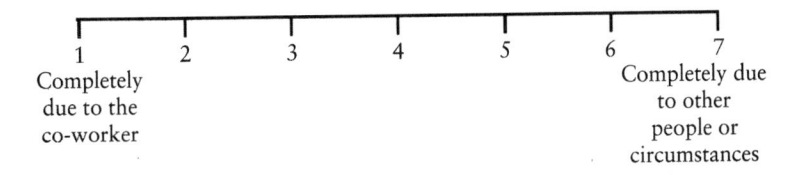

```
┌───┬───┬───┬───┬───┬───┐
1   2   3   4   5   6   7
Completely                      Completely due
due to the                      to other
co-worker                       people or
                                circumstances
```

f. To what extent will the reasons the co-worker did not receive the promotion:

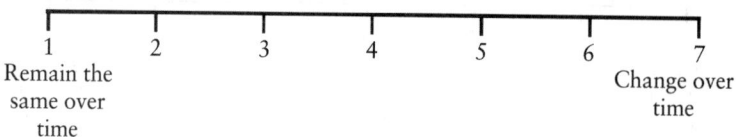

```
  1       2       3       4       5       6       7
Remain the                                    Change over
same over                                        time
time
```

2. Imagine that you have been just been told that a typical co-worker will not receive the raise he or she was hoping to receive.

   To what extent do you believe that each of the following factors would have contributed to the co-worker not receiving the desired raise?

   a. Lack of Ability

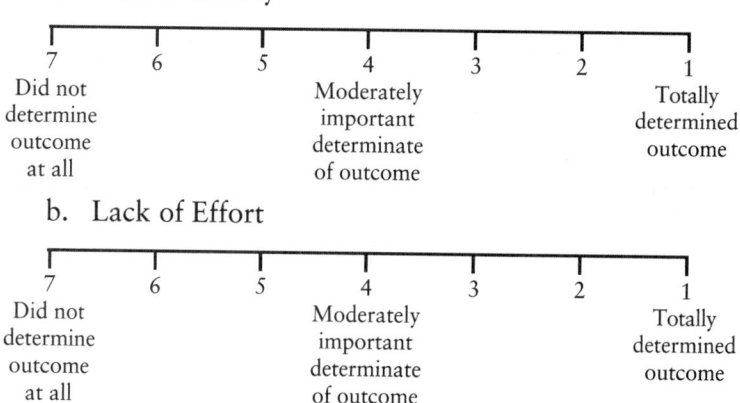

```
  7       6       5       4       3       2       1
Did not                Moderately                Totally
determine              important              determined
outcome                determinate              outcome
at all                 of outcome
```

   b. Lack of Effort

```
  7       6       5       4       3       2       1
Did not                Moderately                Totally
determine              important              determined
outcome                determinate              outcome
at all                 of outcome
```

   c. The Difficulty of getting a raise

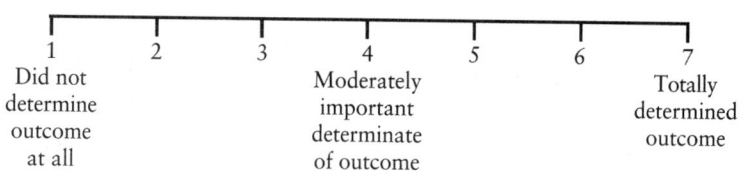

```
  1       2       3       4       5       6       7
Did not                Moderately                Totally
determine              important              determined
outcome                determinate              outcome
at all                 of outcome
```

   d. Bad Luck

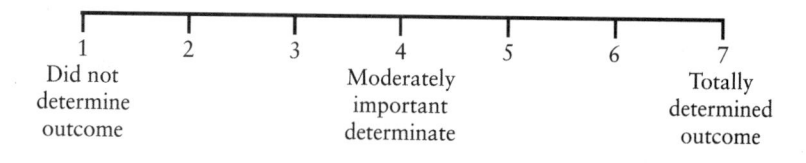

```
  1       2       3       4       5       6       7
Did not                Moderately                Totally
determine              important              determined
outcome                determinate              outcome
```

e. To what extent are the reasons the co-worker did not receive the raise due to something about the co-worker or due to other people or circumstances?

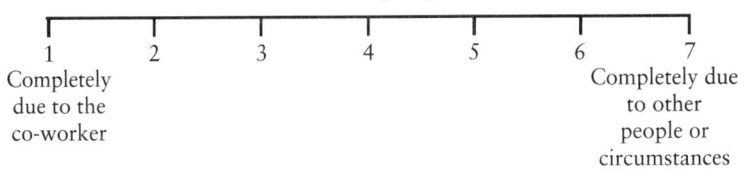

```
    1         2         3         4         5         6         7
Completely                                                Completely due
due to the                                                   to other
co-worker                                                  people or
                                                          circumstances
```

f. To what extent will the reasons the co-worker did not receive the raise:

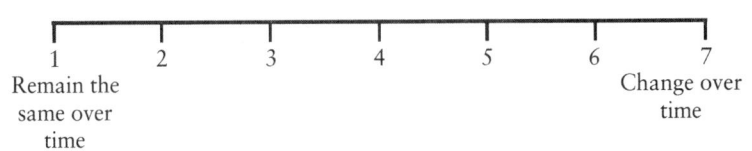

```
    1         2         3         4         5         6         7
Remain the                                                Change over
same over                                                     time
   time
```

3. Imagine that you have been just been told that a typical co-worker will receive the promotion that the co-worker was hoping to receive.

   To what extent do you believe that each of the following factors would have contributed to the co-worker receiving the desired promotion?

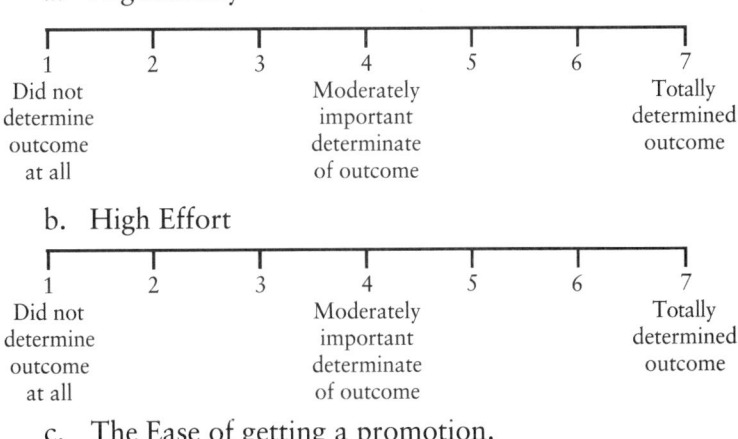

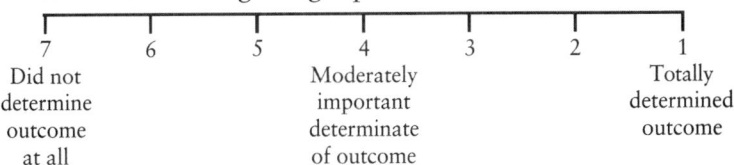

   a. High Ability

```
    1         2         3         4         5         6         7
  Did not             Moderately                            Totally
determine              important                          determined
 outcome              determinate                          outcome
  at all              of outcome
```

   b. High Effort

```
    1         2         3         4         5         6         7
  Did not             Moderately                            Totally
determine              important                          determined
 outcome              determinate                          outcome
  at all              of outcome
```

   c. The Ease of getting a promotion.

```
    7         6         5         4         3         2         1
  Did not             Moderately                            Totally
determine              important                          determined
 outcome              determinate                          outcome
  at all              of outcome
```

d. Good Luck

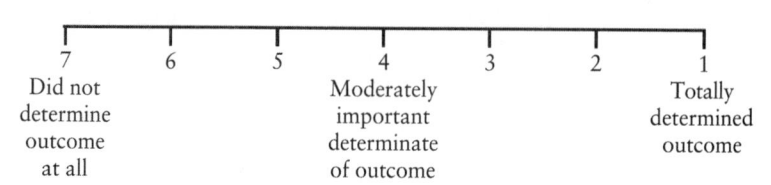

```
┌─────┬─────┬─────┬─────┬─────┬─────┬─────┐
7     6     5     4     3     2     1
Did not           Moderately          Totally
determine         important           determined
outcome           determinate         outcome
at all            of outcome
```

e. To what extent are the reasons the co-worker received the promotion due to something about the co-worker or due to other people or circumstances?

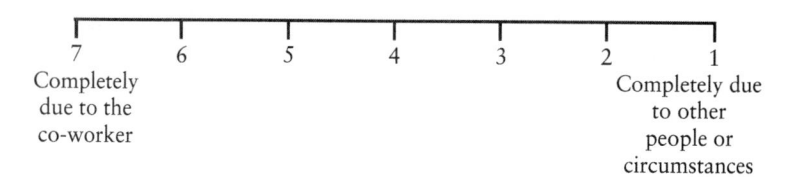

```
┌─────┬─────┬─────┬─────┬─────┬─────┬─────┐
7     6     5     4     3     2     1
Completely                            Completely due
due to the                            to other
co-worker                             people or
                                      circumstances
```

f. To what extent will the reasons the co-worker received the promotion:

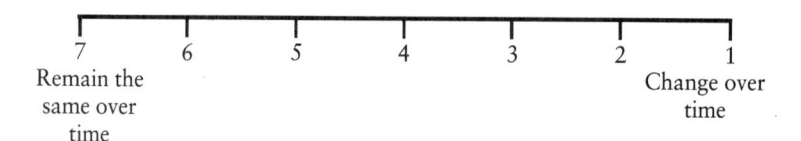

```
┌─────┬─────┬─────┬─────┬─────┬─────┬─────┐
7     6     5     4     3     2     1
Remain the                            Change over
same over                             time
time
```

4. Imagine that you have just been told that a typical co-worker will receive the raise the co-worker has been expecting.

   To what extent do you believe that each of the following factors would have contributed to the co-worker receiving the desired raise?

   a. High Ability

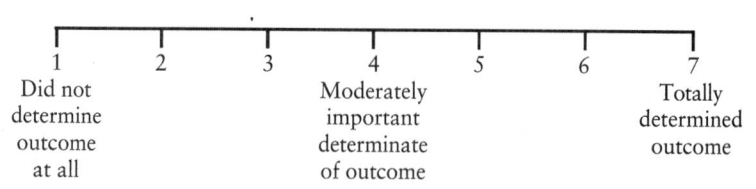

```
┌─────┬─────┬─────┬─────┬─────┬─────┬─────┐
1     2     3     4     5     6     7
Did not           Moderately          Totally
determine         important           determined
outcome           determinate         outcome
at all            of outcome
```

b. High Effort

```
1       2       3       4       5       6       7
Did not                 Moderately              Totally
determine               important               determined
outcome                 determinate             outcome
at all                  of outcome
```

c. The Ease of getting a raise

```
7       6       5       4       3       2       1
Did not                 Moderately              Totally
determine               important               determined
outcome                 determinate             outcome
at all                  of outcome
```

d. Good Luck

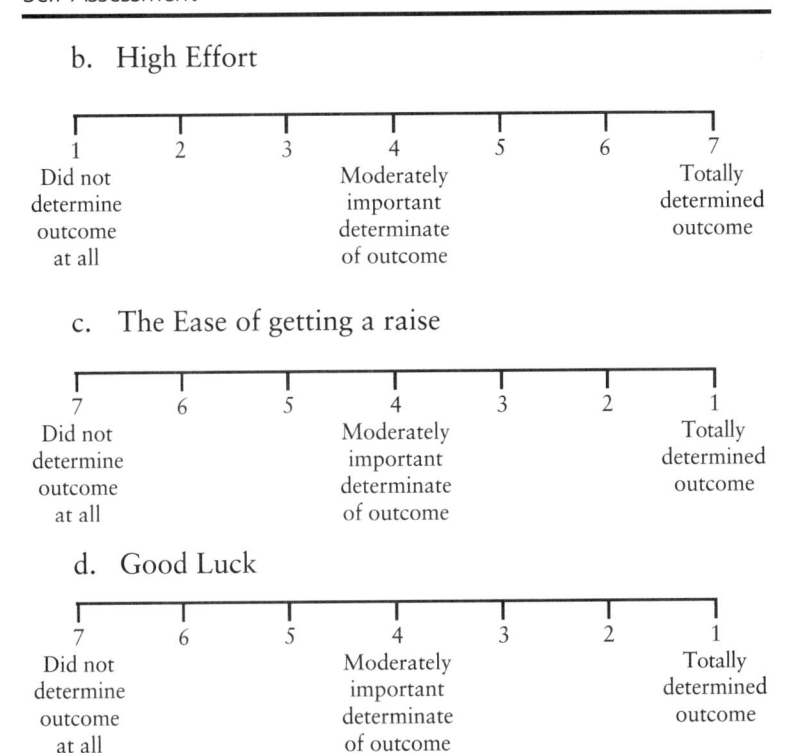

```
7       6       5       4       3       2       1
Did not                 Moderately              Totally
determine               important               determined
outcome                 determinate             outcome
at all                  of outcome
```

e. To what extent are the reasons the co-worker received the raise due to something about the co-worker or due to other people or circumstances?

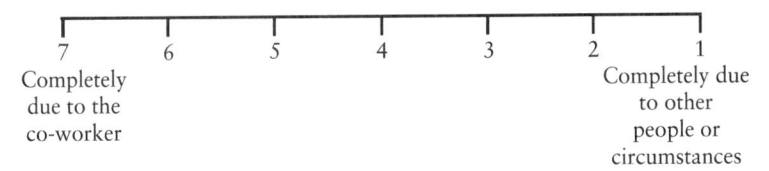

```
7           6       5       4       3       2       1
Completely                                          Completely due
due to the                                          to other
co-worker                                           people or
                                                    circumstances
```

f. To what extent will the reasons the co-worker received the raise:

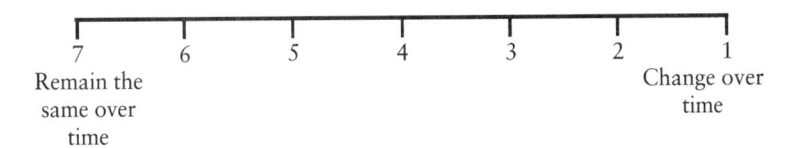

```
7           6       5       4       3       2       1
Remain the                                          Change over
same over                                           time
time
```

Thank you for completing the self-assessment. It was important to take the test before beginning the discussion of causal reasoning so that you would not bias your answers when taking the test. Procedures for scoring the self-test will be discussed later in the book.

CHAPTER III

CAUSAL REASONING

The notion that the way people think about their successes and failures affects their future behavior and motivation has been studied for years. The various labels that have been applied to this type of research include attribution theory, cognitive appraisal theory, behavioral decision-making theory, schematic and categorical decision-making, and theories of causal reasoning. For the most part, these theories complement rather than contradict one another. For the purpose of our discussion, these theories will be referred to as Causal Reasoning (CR) theory.

The basic premise of CR theory is that in order to survive, people have an innate need to understand the causes of their successes and failures. Based on their beliefs (i.e., attributions) regarding the causes of their successes and failures, individuals then alter their behavior to achieve success and avoid failure. More specifically, research has demonstrated that when people succeed or fail, they often attribute the outcome to a cause such as ability, the difficulty of the task, effort, or luck. These, of course, are the same explanations that we assessed with the short quiz in the previous chapter. Using the short quiz as an example, you can see that, for most people, attributing failure to a lack of ability is a problem, since most people view their ability as fixed and unchanging. Thus, when individuals attribute failure to inability, which they believe will not change, they are unlikely to exert effort in the future. Furthermore, research demonstrates that when individuals attribute a failure to low ability, they often become depressed and experience learned helplessness, a condition in which people simply give up and quit trying.

Attributing failure to lack of effort is much more functional since effort can change and is therefore a solvable problem. Typically, when failure is attributed to a lack of effort, the individual tries harder in the future.

Attributing failure to the difficulty of the task (i.e., the situation) is not as debilitating as attributing failure to a lack of ability, since it generally does not affect self-esteem. Nonetheless, when individuals believe that they can't win, they often give up.

As in the case of task attributions, attributing failure to luck and chance does not erode the individual's self-esteem and, more importantly, individuals may choose to continue to try with the belief that luck is capricious and will be on their side, eventually. As the saying goes, "the harder I try, the luckier I get." Using our introductory case as an example, Greg Norman's attribution can be classified into the category of luck and chance (i.e., everybody's game has ups and downs) and, assuming that he gave the media a completely candid response, the loss should not have affected his self-esteem. Although it was left unsaid, one can bet that Greg Norman believes he has the ability (i.e., ability attribution) to win the Masters and that he knows that if he continues to practice and compete (i.e., expend effort), he has a chance (i.e., luck) to win this very difficult (i.e., task difficulty) event.

ATTRIBUTION STYLES AND DIMENSIONS

Research has demonstrated that people have consistent patterns of thinking about success and failure. These patterns are called attribution styles. It has also been found that attributional explanations such as the ones suggested above (i.e., ability, luck, effort, and task difficulty) have underlying dimensional characteristics that can serve as a means for

		STABILITY	
		UNSTABLE	STABLE
L O C U S	INTERNAL	Effort	Ability
	EXTERNAL	Chance/Luck	Type of Task

FIGURE 3.1. Attributional Dimensions and Explanations for Outcomes

classifying attributions (See Figure 3.1). Most attributional explanations (i.e., causes) can be classified as internal (i.e., residing in the person) or external (i.e., residing outside the person). Generally, when people attribute their outcomes to ability and effort, they are identifying themselves as the major causal factor (i.e., internal). On the other hand, when success or failure is attributed to the nature of a task or to luck, the cause is generally perceived by the person as outside of himself or herself (i.e., external). If you check your responses to the self-test, you will find that, in most cases, whenever you made strong ability or effort attributions (questions a & b), you tended to circle a number toward the internal half of the internal/external scale (question e). On the other hand, when you attributed success or failure to the task or to luck (questions c & d), you usually also circled a number on the external end of the internal/external scale (question e).

A second dimension into which the majority of attributional explanations can be categorized is stability, which indicates whether or not the cause is perceived as something that is relatively permanent and stable as opposed to temporary and changing. Luck and effort are generally viewed as changing and unstable whereas ability and the nature of a task are generally viewed as stable and unchanging.

These underlying dimensions are important because they are related to the way people feel about themselves and their expectations of success in the future. The internal/external dimension affects how people feel. When you blame yourself for failure, you are likely to be disappointed and on occasion, may even become depressed. On the other hand, external attributions for failure place the responsibility for the failure outside of oneself. External attributions sometimes result in hostility or aggression directed toward the perceived cause of the failure. Some of our most recent research suggests that individuals who commit acts of organizational violence demonstrate a tendency to make external attributions.

The stability dimension is important because it affects a person's expectations regarding future success. As a general rule, people expect to succeed in the future when they make stable internal (e.g., ability) or stable external (e.g., task difficulty) attributions for past successes. They also believe that they have a chance of succeeding when they make unstable internal (e.g., effort) or unstable external attributions (e.g., luck) for their past failures. On the other hand, people are generally unmotivated and expect failure if they believe that their past failures were due to stable internal or stable external factors, such as lack of ability or an extremely difficult task, respectively.

By combining the stability and internal/external dimensions, we can describe attribution styles, which are consistent patterns of thinking about success and failure. A person with an optimistic attribution style has a tendency to attribute success to internal and stable factors such as ability and a tendency to attribute failure to external and unstable factors such as bad luck. On the other hand, a person with a pessimistic style tends to attribute success to external and unstable factors such as luck and chance while attributing failure to internal and stable factors such as inadequate ability. Put another way, the optimistic individual tends to take credit for success and blame failure on bad luck or chance whereas the pessimist has a tendency to blame failure on personal inadequacies (i.e., low ability) and fails to take credit for success, attributing success to unstable outside factors (e.g., luck and chance). Research in the area of mental health has demonstrated that people with pessimistic styles often become depressed and sometimes suffer from debilitating helplessness, because they feel that they have little control over their lives.

POTENTIAL ATTRIBUTION STYLES

Although optimistic and pessimistic attribution styles are most commonly discussed in the research, all possible combinations of the dimensions of internality/externality and stability/instability yield the sixteen potential styles that will be discussed in Chapter Seven. Because the research has focused primarily on optimistic and pessimistic styles, we know the most about these two styles. Therefore, in order to illustrate how attribution styles influence behavior and expectations, we will concentrate on a thorough description of the optimistic and pessimistic styles in the next two chapters. After that, we will discuss the results of the self-tests that you took in Chapter Two. Then we will discuss all sixteen of the styles and the question of which style or styles are optimal for success.

DEFINITIONS

Causal Reasoning (CR) Theory—a label for the set of theories that explains how people think about their successes and failures. CR theories include attribution theory, cognitive appraisal theory, and schematic and categorical decision-making theories.

Attribution—A causal explanation for success or failure.

Explanation—the specific reason an individual gives for a particular success or failure. Typical explanations include ability, luck, effort, and the difficulty of a task or situation.

Dimensions—categories that can serve as a means for classifying attributions (e.g., internal/external and stable/unstable).

Attribution styles—consistent patterns of thinking about success and failure.

Pessimistic attribution style—the tendency of some individuals to attribute failure to internal and stable characteristics (e.g., low ability) and attribute success to external and unstable factors (e.g., luck and chance).

Optimistic attribution style—the tendency of some individuals to make internal and stable attributions for success (e.g., high ability) and attribute failures to unstable external dimensions such as luck and chance.

KEY POINTS

1. The way people think about their successes and failures affects their future behavior and motivation.
2. A basic premise of CR theory is that in order to survive, people have an innate need to understand the causes of their successes and failures.
3. When failure is attributed to a lack of ability, which does not change, people are unlikely to exert effort in the future.
4. When failure is attributed to a lack of effort, which can change, people usually try harder in the future if they value the outcome.
5. When failure is attributed to an impossible situation or task, which will not change, people often give up because they believe they cannot win.
6. When failure is attributed to luck and chance it does not erode self-esteem and people usually continue to try with the belief that luck can change and will eventually be on their side.
7. Most attributions can be classified as internal (causes residing within the person) or external (causes in the environment outside the person).
8. The internal/external dimension affects how people feel.
9. Internal attributions for failure often lead to negative feelings about the self (e.g., guilt and shame) whereas external attributions for failure place the responsibility for failure outside of the self and can result in negative

feelings (e.g., hostility and blame) directed toward the perceived cause of the failure.

10. Internal attributions for success usually lead to good feelings (e.g., increased confidence and self-esteem) and continued efforts to achieve success.

11. Most attributions can also be classified as stable or unstable, which indicates the degree to which causes will remain the same or are likely to change.

12. People are generally unmotivated and expect failure if they believe that their past failures were due to stable factors.

13. People generally persist in motivated behavior when they believe that their successes are due to stable factors.

14. All possible combinations of the dimensions of internality/externality and stability/instability yield sixteen potential styles.

CHAPTER IV

THE ARCHETYPAL OPTIMIST

Johnny Simmons was the kind of guy people liked to be around. He had been a big time contractor for commercial buildings. But when I met him he was down and out after both his business and marriage went south at the same time. All he had left was the family beach house (which his wife couldn't take) and I was one of the many guests he invited for the weekend. Despite the fact that he was completely broke, the doors and windows were wide open, the air conditioning ran at full blast (you could hang meat inside), there was plenty to eat and drink, and there was a constant party and stream of friends. Johnny and his friends drank, partied, and reminisced about the "good years" when he would have lobsters flown in from Maine, serve three-inch steaks, and ten-count shrimp with Absolut, Jack Daniels, and Crown Royale. Johnny could tell a story and he frequently reminisced about his friends and exploits. Some of his favorite stories were about his employees and in particular, his favorite "go-fer" who called himself Dallas. Dallas was a North Florida redneck who had never been more than 50 miles from home and adopted his nickname to convince people he was a real cowboy. Dallas told stories of jumping out of trees and slitting the throats of unsuspecting deer, breaking a wild mustang, and wiping out seven people in a bar fight. Dallas also claimed to be a Ninja expert and Johnny loved to tell the story where Dallas brought his numchucks to the job and knocked himself out during a demonstration. Despite the mistakes that Dallas made, along with the many other incompetent employees that Johnny had surrounded himself with, it was apparent that Johnny loved his people with their faults. There never was a mean twist to the stories.

Johnny was remarkable in many other ways. I first met him when he was at the bottom and he stayed there for five years, letting his life and property deteriorate. He loved to fish offshore and had a 38-ft. Bertram he called "Absolut Fun" after his favorite brand of vodka. His banker, Randy, frequently called Johnny about the loan on the boat. Finally, Johnny went to the Bahamas and left the boat there. Johnny had a saying, "A banker is your friend until you need one," and he treated Randy with disdain. When Randy went to repossess Absolut Fun, Johnny simply told him he didn't have the boat and didn't know where it was. As far as I know, nothing ever happened to Johnny because of the boat and I'm still not sure the bank ever got the boat back. Johnny must have had something on Randy who later lost his job after having an affair with his secretary who was the daughter of one of the bank's officers.

As I began to know Johnny, at first it was hard to imagine how he had ever been so successful. He always called me "Doc," which conveyed a kind of disdainful respect for a Yankee with a Ph.D. On the very few occasions when I would ask him what happened to his business (no one else would dare ask him), he would look at me as if I were simple-minded and brush away the subject. He attributed his failure to a change in the economy. He said there was a recession and his business was one of the casualties. Simple as that. He offered similar explanations for his marriage. His wife was greedy and when the money and fun ran out, she also ran out. None of Johnny's failures were ever Johnny's fault.

Over time as I became more familiar with Johnny and CR theory was developing, I began to realize that Johnny was the personification of the archetypal optimist. When he failed, it was always due to someone or something else beside himself. Johnny was not given to self-analysis and, at times, it appeared that he was incapable of any type of deep analytical thinking. He seemed uncomfortable in one-on-one situations but was the life of the party when he was in a group. On the other hand, I never saw Johnny depressed and never saw even the slightest indication of self-doubt. Regarding success, he always said he had done it before and would do it again. He took full and complete responsibility for his success.

Johnny never changed but his life underwent an awesome transformation before he died. After his divorce and bankruptcy allowed him to clear the slate, he remarried. Establishing a business and credit in his wife's name, he took their joint net worth which was probably less than $30,000 and, within three years, parlayed it into a new construction business that was grossing more than a million dollars a year and netting close to $400,000. In his last year, Johnny cleared over one million, after less than six years in business.

The same set of attributions that contributed to Johnny's remarkable turn-around also probably cost him his life. By his early fifties, Johnny's diet of red meat and Absolut caught up with him and at least one of the arteries to his heart was estimated to be 80% blocked. Johnny only knew this after he collapsed and was taken to the emergency ward. Johnny was counseled regarding diet, exercise, and angioplasty. But, Johnny loved fishing, hated doctors almost as much as he hated bankers, and it was tournament time. Every year he participated in a billfish tournament with the same core group of characters. The Nassau (i.e., side) bets often exceeded the tournament prize of $500,000. After a long day of fishing, which included a two-hour fight with a marlin that was unsuccessful, Johnny hit the dock and tried to overcome the weakness he felt with filet mignon and Absolut. He had a heart attack and was life-flighted to the hospital. He lasted two days but eventually his liver and kidneys failed along with his heart. He was able to talk to one or two close friends. His message was that he had had a good ride and no regrets. Even at the end, Johnny did not appear to perceive that personal causation had anything to do with his problems. At the end he told his young wife, "I may be checking out a few years early but I've had ten times more fun than anyone I know."

I'm not like Johnny, but I have to honestly say I learned to respect him. He always had a good time, everybody loved him (with a few very hostile exceptions), and, at least as far as I could tell, he never spent a depressing moment. He was the epitome of an optimist and attributed his success to internal and stable characteristics (e.g., his ability, good looks, charisma, etc.) and exuded confidence as a result. On the other hand, he attributed his failures to external and unstable characteristics such as the changing economy, bad luck, and people that he couldn't trust.

CHAPTER V

THE PESSIMISTIC CR STYLE

It's a bit more difficult to paint an endearing picture of the pessimist. Pessimists are people who never experience the joy of success because they believe that success is due to temporary (i.e., unstable) causes such as luck. On the other hand, pessimists know the agony of defeat because they attribute failure to their own internal and stable characteristics such as low ability.

Considerable insight into the nature and development of pessimistic attitudes can be gained by examining the early research on learned helplessness. The early studies were done in psychological laboratories with animals. While you may have some reservations as to whether or not animal studies can apply to humans, I believe that once you have read the explanation of the work that follows, combined with the subsequent research on humans, you will find that this group of studies is helpful in understanding how and why some people, when faced with challenges, demonstrate frustration and helplessness whereas others, who experience the same challenges, remain calm, optimistic, and motivated.

The initial work on learned helplessness began as a series of studies investigating learning in dogs by Martin Seligman and his colleagues. In these studies, a dog would be placed in a two-way shuttle box. The box was constructed with a small barrier between two sections. One side of the grid in the box was electrified and the other side was safe.

The dogs were tethered to the electrified grid so they could not move to the safe side of the box. On the first trial, a light would go on and, shortly afterwards, the dogs would receive a shock. At first, the dogs whined, howled, and attempted to escape to the safe side of the box. Over time, they learned that they could not escape the shock and when the light that signaled the shock went on, the dogs remained passive and no longer attempted to escape. In later experiments, the researchers found that once the dogs were conditioned, even when the restraints were removed, many of the dogs remained passive and failed to escape. The notion that individuals become passive after a series of bad experiences and remain passive even though the situation and conditions change, making success possible, has been labeled learned helplessness.

Later research demonstrated that the same types of helpless behaviors are found in people. Within business environments, for example, many individuals who have bad experiences with information technologies demonstrate helplessness when they are forced to adopt a new information technology. Similarly, many consumers who experienced the poor quality of many cars that were manufactured in the United States during the 1970s have learned helplessness and will not buy another U.S.-made car, despite the fact that the quality of U.S.-made cars has improved. Finally, another example is managers who have a history of belittling employees and disregarding their input. When these managers try to change their styles and encourage employee input, their employees are often reluctant to provide feedback since they were punished frequently in the past and do not recognize that the manager has changed.

While it is possible to point to many other examples of learned helplessness, the key question however is, "Given the same situation, why do some people experience helplessness whereas others remain motivated and persistent?" Later research found that, at least with the human subjects, the key difference was how they thought about the process. Those who made pessimistic attributions and attributed their negative outcomes to their own internal and stable deficiencies such as lack of ability were much more likely to become depressed and experience helplessness. On the other hand, more optimistic individuals who blamed their negative experiences on external factors such as chance and luck generally did not experience helplessness and depression. Over time, the work on attribution theory and learned helplessness (i.e., CR theory) became the foundation for a major theoretical explanation of human depression. It is now recognized that pessimistic attribution styles often lead to depression and a variety of dysfunctional behaviors including a lack of persistence, poor performance, absenteeism, turnover, and drug and alcohol abuse.

In a recent book by Martin Seligman, it was suggested that optimistic styles are generally more healthy and functional than pessimistic styles. Some of this research supports the notion that pessimistic styles, which often lead to learned helplessness and depression, are related to poor performance. However, the research on optimistic styles has not shown that optimistic styles are unequivocally more effective than other styles. Consider for a moment what style would probably be more effective for a banker: an optimistic or pessimistic style. Clearly, a pronounced optimistic style wherein the banker would attribute failures to external and unstable factors such as chance and luck would be counterproductive. On the other hand, research has demonstrated that optimistic styles are associated with the success of insurance salespeople as well as with the adoption of new information technologies. And indeed logic supports this finding. Certainly, when a saleswoman has the door slammed in her face, she is less likely to be disappointed if she makes an optimistic attribution (e.g., external and unstable—a crabby customer) as opposed to a pessimistic internal and stable attribution (e.g., I have no sales ability). Similarly, when an attempt to apply a new information technology fails, the user is more likely to try again in the future if he makes an external unstable attribution (e.g., temporary problem with the new system) as opposed to an internal an stable attribution (e.g., I'm no good and I'll never be any good at these types of things).

Given the above examples, the question still remains, "What is the most effective style?" Before trying to provide a definitive answer to this question, it will be helpful to take a look at the answers to the self-test to see which type of style your responses suggested.

DEFINITIONS

Learned helplessness—the notion that individuals become passive after a series of punishing experiences and remain passive even though the situation and conditions change making success possible.

KEY POINTS

1. The major reason some people experience helplessness whereas others remain motivated in the same situation is the way they think about the process.

2. Pessimistic individuals who attribute their negative outcomes to their own internal and stable characteristics such as lack of ability are much more likely than others to become depressed and experience helplessness.

3. Optimistic individuals who blame their negative experiences on external dimensions such as chance and luck, generally do not experience helplessness and depression.

4. Pessimistic attribution styles often lead to depression and a variety of dysfunctional behaviors including a lack of persistence, poor performance, absenteeism, turnover, and drug and alcohol abuse.

CHAPTER VI

INTERPRETING THE SELF-TEST
PART I

Now that we have had a chance to see how optimistic and pessimistic CR styles affect behavior, it will be meaningful to take a look at the results of Part I of the self-test. These results will help you to examine your own particular CR style. Several caveats are in order before discussing the self-test. First, the short questionnaire is only an indication of your potential CR style. Although similar questions on prior CR style tests appear to be valid and reliable indications of CR style, the brevity of this questionnaire and the conditions under which it was taken (i.e., a self-test) make it difficult for one to be completely confident that it is reliable and valid. Nonetheless, the self-test is useful in suggesting what your CR style may be. Second, although measures of CR styles are useful in predicting individuals' thought patterns, emotions, and behaviors, the actual situation with which you are confronted is usually more predictive of how you will interpret the situation and how you will react. More specifically, CR styles represent tendencies to think in a particular way and people do not always follow their tendencies. For example, even the most pessimistic person will blame the other driver if he or she is rear-ended when stopped at a traffic light.

Thus, CR styles only suggest tendencies and do not predict how an individual will respond in a specific situation. However, over the long haul, the consistent biases represented by CR styles will have an impact. Thus, the interpretations of the self-test that are provided in this chapter should help to demonstrate the tendencies you may have, but they should not be interpreted as predicting what your response will be in all situations.

The procedures for scoring the self-test and the interpretations of the scores are provided below.

LOC SCORES

Locus of Causality (LOC) scores indicate the degree to which you attribute your successes and failures to internal characteristics such as your ability and effort as opposed to external causes such as a difficult or easy situation or luck and chance. High internals take responsibility for their outcomes whereas high externals attribute their successes and failures to factors outside of themselves. The scores on this dimension are also important because they are related to how you feel about yourself. High internals are particularly proud of themselves when they succeed but often blame themselves for failures. High externals, on the other hand, do not feel as much personal responsibility for either their successes or failures. As the scoring procedures below suggest, not all people are one-dimensional and some may attribute success internally while attributing failure to external causes.

In the first questionnaire that you took there were two success and two failure events. Items 1 and 2 assessed how you responded to failure events. Items 3 and 4 assessed how you reacted to success. You can determine your own score by following the directions below.

LOC Scores for Success Events

Calculate the LOC scores for positive events by adding up the scores for the following items:

3a. ____ + 3b. ____ + 3c ____ + 3d. ____ + 3e. ____
+ 4a. ____ + 4b. ____ + 4c. ____ + 4d. ____ + 4e. ____
= Total ____

CIRCLE

> INTERNAL FOR SUCCESS EVENTS (if your score is above 35)
>
> EXTERNAL FOR SUCCESS EVENTS (if your score is 35 or below)

This score should be between 10 and 70 and indicates the degree to which you take credit for success and is an indication of optimism. In general, if your score is above 35, you are a high internal positive meaning that you take credit for your successes and success makes you feel good about yourself. If your score is 35 or below, you are a high external positive and you may have a tendency to be uncomfortable with success and tend to credit the situation or others when you succeed.

LOC Scores for Failure Events

Calculate the LOC scores for negative events by adding up the scores for the following items:

1a. ____ + 1b. ____ + 1c. ____ + 1d. ____ + 1e. ____
+ 2a ____ + 2b. ____ +2c. ____ + 2d. ____ + 2e. ____
= Total ____

CIRCLE

> EXTERNAL FOR FAILURE EVENTS (if your score is above 35)
>
> INTERNAL FOR FAILURE EVENTS (if your score is 35 or below)

This score should also be between 10 and 70 and indicates the degree to which you blame yourself for failure and is an indication of pessimism. In general, if your score is below 35, you have a strong tendency to make internal attributions for negative events meaning that you tend to blame yourself when things go wrong. As a result, it is likely that you feel very bad about yourself when you fail. On the other hand, if your score is above 35, you tend to make external attributions for negative events. Thus you do not internalize failure but tend to blame negative outcomes on something or someone beside yourself. The assets of the tendency to make internal attributions for negative events are that the individual takes responsibility for negative outcomes. The liability is that these individuals tend to blame themselves too much and may become so depressed they are ineffectual. On the other hand, the liability of individuals who tend to make external attributions for negative events is that they fail to take responsibility for their failures and may then fail to take necessary corrective actions. The positive side of this tendency is that, because they do not blame themselves for failure, people who make external attributions for negative events are less likely to become discouraged and feel bad about themselves and may be more persistent than their more internal counterparts.

STABILITY SCORES

Stability scores are important because they are an indication of whether or not the person believes the cause of an outcome is permanent or temporary. If the cause of a negative outcome is believed to be stable and permanent as in the case of low ability, the person does not expect that additional effort will lead to a different outcome in the future. On the other hand, if the cause of a negative event is believed to be unstable and temporary as in the case of luck and chance, the person expects that continuing to try can be worthwhile because luck changes. Similarly, stable attributions for success increase the expectancy of future success whereas unstable attributions for success decrease expectations that future effort will pay off. Thus the stability dimension affects your expectations of future success whereas the LOC dimension described previously affects your emotions and how you feel about yourself.

Please follow the directions below to calculate your stability scores:

Stability Scores for Success Events

Calculate the stability score for positive events by adding up the scores for the following items:

3a._____ -3b._____ -3c._____ +3d._____ + 3f._____
+ 4a._____ - 4b._____ -4c._____ + 4d._____ + 4f._____
= Total _____

Scores should range from -11 to +19.

CIRCLE

    STABLE FOR SUCCESS EVENTS (if your score is above 4)

    UNSTABLE FOR SUCCESS EVENTS (if your score is 4 or below)

This score, as indicated above, suggests the degree to which you believe that your successes are due to stable causes such as your ability. In general, if your score is above 4, you believe that when you experience positive events, they are caused by stable factors. Because of your belief in the stability of these causes, you also expect that you will also be successful in similar situations in the future. If your score is below 4, you tend to believe that the causes of your successes are due to unstable factors such as high effort or luck and you tend to lack confidence that you will be successful in the future. Thus you may give up and quit trying since you don't expect to succeed.

Clearly, stable attributions for success indicate a more optimistic attribution style while attributing success to unstable causes is more pessimistic.

Stability Score for Failure Events

Calculate the stability score for failure events by adding up the scores for the following items:

-1a._____ + 1b._____ + 1c._____ -1d._____ - 1f._____
-2a._____ +2b._____ +2c._____ - 2d._____ - 2f._____
= Total _____

Scores should range from -38 to +22.

CIRCLE

UNSTABLE FOR NEGATIVE EVENTS (if your score is above -8)

STABLE FOR NEGATIVE EVENTS (if your score is -8 or below)

As discussed above, this score suggests the degree to which you believe that your failures are due to stable causes such as your ability. In general, if your score is below -8, you indicated that when you experienced the negative events described by the questionnaire, they were caused by stable factors. Because of your tendency to believe that the causes of your failures are stable and enduring, you also expect that you will have difficulty achieving success in similar situations in the future. If your score is above -8, you tend to believe that the causes of your failures are due to unstable factors such as low effort or luck and you tend to believe that you will eventually achieve success because things can be different in the future. Thus you have a tendency to persist in behavior that has not been productive because you think that situations and circumstances may change in the future.

OVERALL ASSESSMENT

By combining the above results you can derive your potential CR style, which will be a combination of the two dimensions of the LOC and stability measures for both the success and failure scenarios. Below, please underline each of the dimensions you circled for each of the four scores that you derived.

1. internal/external for success events.
2. internal/external for failure events.
3. stable/unstable for success events
4. stable/unstable for failure events.

Your potential type will correspond to one of the CR types discussed in the next chapter.

KEY POINTS

1. The short questionnaire is only an indication of your potential CR style.

2. CR styles indicate tendencies and do not predict how an individual will respond in a specific situation.

3. Over the long haul, the consistent biases represented by CR styles will have an impact.

CHAPTER VII

THE SIXTEEN CAUSAL REASONING TYPES

At the onset, please understand that, for the most part, current literature and theory only describe the pessimistic (internal and stable for failure/ external and unstable for success) and optimistic (internal and stable for success/ external and unstable for failure) styles. Thus, the descriptions of the other styles suggested in Table 7.1 are based on the logic of the theory rather than research that demonstrates the characteristics of people with these styles. Although speculating about the nature of these styles may make some of my academic colleagues uncomfortable, it is probably the best way to begin thinking about how the combinations of the different attributional dimensions interact. Thus, the descriptions that are offered below are tentative. They are useful to theorists in that empirical testing could be conducted to test whether or not people who test a particular way actually behave the way the descriptions suggest. For our purposes, they are useful in that they can help you think about the style you have and how it may be affecting your behavior, your interpersonal relations, and your motivation to achieve.

MR. OR MS. RESPONSIBLE

People with this style tend to believe that their successes are the result of internal and stable characteristics such as exceptional ability and tend to feel very good about themselves

TABLE 7.1. POTENTIAL ATTRIBUTION STYLES

	SUCCESS ATTRIBUTIONS	FAILURE ATTRIBUTIONS
1. MR. OR MS. RESPONSIBLE	INTERNAL/STABLE (E.G., ABILITY)	INTERNAL/STABLE (E.G., LACK OF ABILITY)
2. THE DOER	INTERNAL/STABLE (E.G., ABILITY)	INTERNAL/UNSTABLE (E.G., LACK OF EFFORT)
3. MS. OR MR. WONDERFUL	INTERNAL/STABLE (E.G., ABILITY)	EXTERNAL/STABLE (E.G., ENVIRONMENT AND OTHER PEOPLE)
4. THE OPTIMIST	INTERNAL/STABLE (E.G., ABILITY)	EXTERNAL/UNSTABLE (E.G., BAD LUCK)
5. THE MARTYR	INTERNAL/UNSTABLE (E.G., EFFORT)	INTERNAL/STABLE (E.G., LACK OF ABILITY)
6. THE SELF-MADE MAN/WOMAN	INTERNAL/UNSTABLE (E.G., EFFORT)	INTERNAL/UNSTABLE (E.G., LACK OF EFFORT)
7. THE POLITICIAN	INTERNAL/UNSTABLE (E.G., EFFORT)	EXTERNAL/STABLE (E.G., ENVIRONMENT AND OTHER PEOPLE)
8. THE VICTIM	INTERNAL/UNSTABLE (E.G., EFFORT)	EXTERNAL/UNSTABLE (E.G., BAD LUCK)

The Sixteen Causal Reasoning Types

9. THE ACCOMMODATOR (PERFECT GUEST)	EXTERNAL/STABLE (E.G., EASE OF TASK)	INTERNAL/STABLE (E.G., LACK OF ABILITY)
10. THE PLUGGER	EXTERNAL/STABLE (E.G., EASE OF TASK)	INTERNAL/UNSTABLE (E.G., LACK OF EFFORT)
11. THE BLAMER	EXTERNAL/STABLE (E.G., EASE OF TASK)	EXTERNAL/STABLE (E.G., ENVIRONMENT AND OTHER PEOPLE)
12. THE HIPPIE (GO WITH THE FLOW)	EXTERNAL/STABLE (E.G., EASE OF TASK)	EXTERNAL/UNSTABLE (E.G., BAD LUCK)
13. THE PESSIMIST	EXTERNAL/UNSTABLE (E.G., GOOD LUCK)	INTERNAL/STABLE (E.G., LACK OF ABILITY)
14. MR. OR MS. TRAGIC	EXTERNAL/UNSTABLE (E.G., GOOD LUCK)	INTERNAL/UNSTABLE (E.G., LACK OF EFFORT)
15. THE DEPENDENT	EXTERNAL/UNSTABLE (E.G., GOOD LUCK)	EXTERNAL/STABLE (E.G., ENVIRONMENT AND OTHER PEOPLE)
16. THE SOCIALITE	EXTERNAL/UNSTABLE (E.G., GOOD LUCK)	EXTERNAL/UNSTABLE (E.G., BAD LUCK)

when things are going well. However, people with this style also tend to make internal and stable attributions for failure, blaming character traits or lack of key abilities, thus they tend to take more personal responsibility than they should for failures. The positive side is that people with this style are often willing to accept responsibility for failure. The negative side is that the people with this style often take themselves too seriously and can be overly critical of themselves when failures occur.

THE DOER

People with this style have a tendency to make internal and stable attributions for success and experience a sense of personal accomplishment when successes occur. On the other hand, people with this style also tend to take personal responsibility for failure by attributing it to internal but unstable characteristics such as inadequate effort. The positive side is that people with this style usually feel good about themselves and are ready to keep on trying even when they encounter failure. The negative side is that people with this style also tend to feel that they can overcome all obstacles by working harder. Thus, people with this style can become fixated and stuck on projects and issues that cannot be resolved through additional effort.

MR. OR MS. WONDERFUL

People with this style often take credit for successes by attributing them to internal and stable characteristics such as ability. On the other hand, they tend to blame their failures on stable and external causes such as other people or an unfair environment. The positive side is that when things are going well, people with this style tend to feel good about themselves. The negative aspect of this style is that people with this style tend not to work to overcome failure because they blame other people or situations for their failures. This configuration of biases is sometimes called the hostile attribution style, because in extreme cases, these types of individuals direct retaliation toward the perceived source of their problems (i.e., other people, society, or an organization). The day-trader who shot fellow trainees at a brokerage firm when the market crashed shortly after New Year's in 2000 is an example of a person who probably had this type of bias.

THE OPTIMIST

Chapter Four described this style in detail. Optimists essentially take credit for success by making internal and stable attributions such as ability and blaming failure on external and unstable factors such as bad luck and chance. The positive side of this style is that optimists are almost never discouraged. An optimist is the kind of salesperson that can go door to door with rejection after rejection, believing that luck will change and the next customer will greet him with open arms. The negative side is that optimists may fail to recognize bad situations or people and remain in circumstances where they are destined to fail.

THE MARTYR

Martyrs tend to attribute success to unstable internal factors such as extraordinary effort. On the other hand, they tend to attribute failure to internal and stable factors such as ability. As a result, they are often depressed, experience feelings of inadequacy, and have low self-esteem. On the positive side, people with this style are often willing to do jobs no one else wants. On the negative side, people with this style tend not to be very adventuresome and because of low self-esteem, they sometimes fail to set challenging goals.

THE SELF-MADE MAN/WOMAN

People with this style tend to believe that internal and unstable attributes such as effort are the cause of both success and failures. Because they tend to believe that extraordinary effort is necessary for success and any lapse in effort will result in failure, they may have a built-in fear of failure and often adopt a workaholic lifestyle. On the positive side, they tend to be proud of their accomplishments and are willing to continue working hard. On the negative side, they rarely stop to smell the roses and often fail to develop a rewarding social life.

THE POLITICIAN

People with this style tend to attribute their successes to internal and unstable causes such as effort and their failures to external and stable causes such as the environment or other people. The upside of this style is that by reading the environment, people with this style can avoid failure and focus their efforts on situations where they can be successful. The downside is that people with this style tend to blame others or the environment for problems that are sometimes caused by themselves. As a result, they may not make the changes they need to make to fully develop their abilities and skills.

THE VICTIM

People with this style tend to make internal and unstable attributions such as extraordinary effort for their successes. Thus, even though they are successful, they may not be confident that they will achieve success in the future because the reasons for their successes are often perceived to be changeable. On the other hand, people with this style tend to attribute their failures to external and unstable factors such as bad luck. Because people with this style tend to view both their successes and failures as caused by factors that are unstable, they have a tendency to be nervous and anxious because they are not confident that they can maintain their good performance. They tend to feel that they are unable to control the factors that have caused their poor performance in the past. On the positive side, people with this style tend to try hard to maintain acceptable performance. On the negative side they often lack the self-confidence necessary to assume positions of responsibility and can get discouraged easily when things are not going well.

THE ACCOMMODATOR

People with this style tend to explain success with external and stable attributions such as an easy task. Thus they are unlikely to experience personal responsibility for success or the feeling of achievement that often accompanies success. On the other hand, they tend to view their failure as due to internal and stable causes such as a lack of ability. On the positive side, people with this style tend to be humble and accommodating. On the negative side, they do not tend to be very achievement oriented.

THE PLUGGER

People with this style tend to attribute their successes to external and stable causes such as an easy task whereas they tend to attribute failures to internal and unstable factors such as a lack of effort. Thus they tend to feel responsible for failure but do not take credit for success. Because they have a tendency to attribute success to stable and external causes, they believe that they can be successful if they "just keep plugging along." The upside of people with this style is that they tend to be fairly reliable employees. The downside is that they tend to have low self-esteem and are not likely to be enthusiastic about themselves or their job.

THE BLAMER

People with this style tend to attribute their successes to external and stable causes such as an easy task and, as a result, do not feel a personal sense of accomplishment when they succeed. On the other hand, when people with this style fail, they also tend to attribute it to causes that are external and stable such as their situation or another person who is not likely to change. On the positive side, people with this style do not tend to be braggadocios or consumed with their personal accomplishments. On the negative side, they tend to whine, blame others for their problems, and lack persistence because they believe that their efforts do not matter.

THE HIPPIE

People with this easy-going style often expect successes because they tend to believe that they are due to external and stable causes such as a benevolent environment or person. When they experience failure, they tend not to be discouraged because they tend to believe it is due to temporary external causes such as bad luck. The upside of people with this style is that they tend to be easy going and assume that things will go well. The downside is that they tend to accept very little responsibility for failure or success and thus are not very achievement oriented because they do not believe that they control their outcomes.

THE PESSIMIST

A thorough explanation of this style and its implications was provided in Chapter Five. In general, people with this style tend to attribute their successes to external and unstable causes such as luck and chance. Therefore, when they experience success it is somewhat unexpected and the person does not feel personally responsible or particularly proud of the accomplishment. On the other hand, pessimists tend to attribute failures to internal and stable causes such as their own lack of ability. Thus, they tend to feel personally responsible for failures and, because they believe the causes are stable, do not expect to succeed in the future. People with this style often experience feelings of depression when they fail.

MR. OR MS. TRAGIC

People with this style tend to attribute their successes to external and unstable causes such as chance and luck. Therefore, they tend to believe that there is little they can do to replicate their success in the future. On the other hand, they tend to believe that their failures are due to unstable and internal causes such as a lack of effort. As a result of this combined perspective of their failures and successes, people with this style exert more effort trying to overcome failures than attempting to replicate and maintain their successes. Because the cause of their failures may often be something other than themselves, they often spend too much time and effort trying to overcome obstacles that are insurmountable. Because they feel little responsibility for success but tend to blame themselves for failure, they tend to have low self-esteem and feel bad about themselves. The upside is that people with this style often persist in the face of obstacles. The downside is that they do not appreciate their talents and often fail to capitalize on their strengths.

THE DEPENDENT

People who display the dependent style tend to attribute successes to external and unstable causes such as luck. Thus, they do not tend to be achievement oriented and are not energized by success since they do not feel any personal responsibility when success occurs. On the other hand, they tend to attribute failures to external and stable causes such as an unhelpful mentor or poor work environment. As a result, they tend to blame failure on other people or circumstances. Because they believe that both their successes and failures are due to causes that are beyond their control (e.g., their supervisor or luck), they tend to exert very little effort to achieve.

THE SOCIALITE

The socialite tends to make external and unstable attributions for success such as luck. Because people with this style do not feel that they have earned their success, they share it with others easily and graciously. Because they also tend to attribute their failure to unstable external causes such as bad luck they do not feel personally threatened or responsible when misfortune occurs. The upside is that people with this style tend to be very sharing with their resources regardless of whether they are wealthy or poor. The downside is that they do little to help their own cause when things are not going well.

CONCLUSION

Once again it is important to emphasize that these descriptions, with the exception of the optimistic and pessimistic styles, are based on theory rather than actual study of people whose assessment placed them in these categories. Thus, the descriptions of the types of behavior and the outcomes associated with the various styles may not be entirely accurate. In addition, to the extent that your scores are not on the high end of the scales, you will be less likely to match the prototypes suggested. Put another way, if your scores were close to the cut-off points for classifying you as internal/external or stable/unstable, your actual type will be more of an amalgamation of several types. Nevertheless, matching your self-assessment scores with the type descriptions hopefully provides a useful tool that enables you to more systematically consider how your CR style affects the way you approach life and how you behave. If you like what you see: GREAT!!! If you don't like what you see, that's okay too. Later chapters contain many suggestions for modifying your style as well as how to influence the styles of others.

CHAPTER VIII

THE EMOTIONALLY INTELLIGENT CAUSAL REASONING STYLE
BOBBY BOWDEN AND NUMBER 11

During the past two decades, my colleagues, students, and I have observed and interviewed more than three hundred successful and unsuccessful leaders to try and identify the factors that differentiate the two groups. At first we hoped that there would be a clear distinction between the traits, behaviors, and CR styles of the successful and less successful managers. We hoped that we would be able to identify one of the sixteen types described in the last chapter as the optimal CR style for managers. However, as the research progressed, it became very clear that neither successful individuals nor successful managers as a group demonstrated consistent traits, behaviors, or CR styles. For the most part, the objective facts of the situation dictated the trait, behavior, or CR process that emerged. Thus, even though a manager might have a generally optimistic causal reasoning style, she might still make an internal attribution for failure when she knows that the failure was her fault. This, of course is important and necessary since ascertaining the cause of a problem is the first step to solving a problem. Thus, the high performers, as well as the other managers, displayed a variety of CR patterns. As the research progressed, it became more apparent that the high performers were simply more able than the average performers in analyzing their environments, objectively identifying causation, and producing the behaviors necessary to solve their problems. Thus they demonstrated emotional intelligence in that they were able to control their biases and overlook their own personal interest so that they could analyze their situations objectively. Stated another way, we all know people who seem to have a "loose screw" (i.e., a set of biases that overshadows everything else they do). The exceptional managers that we interviewed had all of their screws tight (i.e., appeared to be emotionally objective as opposed to biased), and seemed almost prescient in their abilities to analyze both their successes and failures. The successful managers were clear and confident when they explained the causes of both their successes and failures. They did not avoid the unpleasant aspects of failure but described them objectively. On the other hand, the less successful managers seemed less willing to talk about failures, and, in particular, appeared to be less objective in their diagnoses of the causes for these failures. Two managers who perhaps best exemplified this prescient causal analysis style were Florida State University coaches Bobby Bowden and Mike Martin.

COACH BOWDEN

Bobby Bowden is arguably the premier coach in college football today. In addition to winning National Championships in 1993 and 1999, Coach Bowden's Florida State Seminoles finished with an Associated Press national ranking of 5th or better for a record 14 consecutive seasons and an NCAA record of 14 consecutive 10-victory seasons. Recently, ESPN honored the Florida State Seminoles as the team of the decade.

In an interview conducted exclusively for this book, I had the opportunity to ask Coach Bowden about his three most memorable successes and failures. In each case, I also asked Coach Bowden to analyze the causes for the successes and failures. It should be emphasized that, at the time, like the other managers who were interviewed for our research, Coach Bowden was not familiar with CR theory or the specifics of this book.

One of the first things that impressed me in the interview with Coach Bowden was my inability to get him to talk in the first person. When asked about his successes and failures, he invariably referred to his team and he almost always said "we", regardless of whether he was talking about winning or losing, although, as we will see later, he did claim personal responsibility for at least one of his major disappointments. Thus, unlike many of today's self-serving leaders who take credit for success and blame others for failure, Bobby's references to "we" clearly indicated that he did not differentiate himself from the team. He shared both the successes and failures with the other coaches and athletes and took more of the blame for failure when he believed that he deserved it.

When asked about his three most memorable successes he identified: 1.) the National Championship in 1993; 2.) beating Michigan at Michigan in 1991; and 3.) beating Pitt at home in the last year he coached at West Virginia. His three most memorable low points were 1.) losing to Pitt at Pitt while leading 35 to 8 at half-time; 2.) losing to Oklahoma in the 1981 Orange Bowl; and 3.) losing to Florida at Florida after beating them four or five times in a row. While these specific incidents are important in and of themselves, it is Coach Bowden's causal analyses of these events that are most revealing about his winning CR style.

Let's take a look at how Bobby Bowden looks at things.

The National Championship Victory

The 1993 National Championship was played at the Orange Bowl in Miami on New Year's Eve. The opponent was the University of Nebraska. On a personal note, I received my doctoral degree from the University of Nebraska in 1977 but had undergone a conversion and was a born again Seminole by 1993. The game had a lot of tension and hype. Florida State had beat Nebraska at their place in 1980 and Nebraska had beat Florida State to win the National Championship in 1992. It was a great setting for the National Championship and it pitted the two premier coaches in college football, Bobby Bowden and Tom Osborne, against one another. Unlike many other rivalries, this one was characterized by respect rather than bad blood. I sat on about the 30-yard line about 20 rows away from my former Ph.D. advisor at the University of Nebraska (who lived next to Tom Osborne) and about the same distance from one of my own doctoral students who was teaching at Florida International University. The game itself, as well as the dynamics that surrounded it, made it the most important one I had ever seen as a spectator.

The game was a struggle of Herculean proportions. Florida State had Heisman Trophy winner Charlie Ward. Nebraska had the Butkus Award winner, Trev Alberts, who was one of the greatest college linebackers to ever play the game. The final score was 17-16 and both teams earned every point. Just about everyone who saw the game said that they were exhausted at the end when Nebraska missed a long attempt for a field goal. Coach Bowden's reaction to winning the National Championship was frank and candid: "The feeling was one of relief, not so much an accomplishment. It was a feeling of relief. It made people quit asking, 'When are you ever going to win a National Championship?'"

When asked about the reasons why the Seminoles were able to win the National Championship, Coach Bowden credited the team's members rather than himself, saying, "The reason for that victory was that we had a gifted football team that had several edges. One of them was Charlie Ward. Another edge was team speed, and we had a solid defense."

When we discussed what could be done in the future to win another National Championship, Coach Bowden was quite reflective in talking about the difference between winning and not winning a National Championship. He described the difference as "sometimes a missed kick. In fact Nebraska missed one on the day we won. We missed one several times when we lost...so a missed kick...could have been something like that ... but the big thing is a breakdown, a mechanical breakdown somewhere...that's the only difference that separates a winner from a loser in a close game...usually an error gets you beat, that's what it is, you don't actually beat people, you go out and lose to them, that's what we coaches say." In addition, Coach Bowden talked about the importance of staying healthy in order to win a National Championship. "Injuries play such a big part in it, and then, of course, you've got the human fallacies working in there. It's not a machine where you can press a button and a six jumps up or go press this button and you get fourteen. It doesn't work that way when you are dealing with human beings. They might do anything. As long as there's that human element in there, there's not much more we can do than what we did." Thus, there was also an almost fatalistic quality in Coach Bowden's analysis of what it takes to win (or keep from losing) a National Championship.

The Defeat at the Orange Bowl to Oklahoma

Coach Bowden's analysis of this earlier loss demonstrates the consistency in his pattern of thinking regardless of whether it is a victory or a loss.

In 1981 Florida State was looking at its first potential National Championship going into the Orange Bowl against Oklahoma. Florida State's program was just starting to come into its own. Although a win over Oklahoma would have resulted in the best record in the country, many Seminole fans were doubtful that they would receive the votes for a National Championship even if Florida State did win. The game was another struggle ending in a narrow margin of victory for Oklahoma: 18-17.

Coach Bowden's reaction to the loss: "Again that's a game in which we had them beat. J.C. Watts, the congressman, led them back to a victory . . . You lose a close game, you go back and see four or five times a game where you could have won it, [but] you lost it. When you get beat bad, you don't do that. But when you get beat close you go back and say, 'gosh if we'd have done this or done that we would have won. Or if we have done this and done that we would have won. Or if we have done this and done that we would have won. Or why didn't we do this or do that.' So, usually after a loss like that you're much more critical of yourself than a big loss. Big losses don't bother me that much. I can lose by 40 points, or 30 points, it don't bother me that much."

When asked to describe the reasons for the loss, Coach Bowden said, "We were well prepared and we played good. Except we couldn't stop them on their last drive. Of all things, we couldn't stop Oklahoma's passing attack. Oklahoma never threw the ball back in those days. They were a wishbone and, on that last drive, where they scored and beat us, they threw every down. We kept waiting for the option, waiting for the option, waiting for the option. It never came. They threw every down. Mainly they beat us because of J.C. Watts...he just took the game in his own hands and won it." Thus, rather than blaming himself or his team for the loss, Coach Bowden was gracious in complimenting the other team and recognizing the outstanding performance of J.C. Watts.

When asked what he learned about avoiding such losses in the future, Coach Bowden was again philosophical, saying that there was little that could be done or that could have been done: "Our game plan was perfect. A couple of interceptions they threw right in our hands. I can still see them step-by-step. Threw one right into our hands." It is notable that although Coach Bowden mentioned the possible interceptions, he said "our hands" rather than blaming any particular individual.

Florida State Loss to the University of Florida—1983

Coach Bowden's analysis of this game demonstrates the consistency in his pattern of thinking about the importance of recruiting and talent. The loss was an important one and it eliminated Florida State from the National Championship picture. As Coach Bowden explained: "They just killed us down there." When asked about his emotional reaction to that loss Coach Bowden said, "That one was terrible because it was a big state rival and they dominated us so bad, we made mistakes, played down there, made a lot of mistakes. They capitalized on it. They beat our brains out; the worst beating we've had by Florida since I've been here."

In the Oklahoma game Coach Bowden gave J.C. Watts a lot of the credit. His analysis of the Florida loss was similar in that he credited the talent of the Florida team. "They had better players. That was one I didn't worry too much about being out-coached. They just had better players. That's when Charley Pell was beginning to hit his stride down there."

Coach Bowden's reaction to what he could do to prevent a similar loss in the future was very straightforward. "We recruited better, drafted better players." Coach Bowden has also elaborated on this theme numerous times in his public appearances. He stresses the notion of impact players, players like J.C. Watts who can take over a game, making the other 21 players on the field seem almost irrelevant. One of his proudest accomplishments each year has to be the media announcement that he has, once again, recruited one of the top five freshman classes in the country. It is also not coincidental that the day after the National Championship victory in the Orange Bowl, he stayed in the Miami area recruiting for the following year's class. Game-breaking impact players like Deion Sanders, Charlie Ward, Brad Johnson, Warrick Dunn, and William Floyd were the result of this philosophy.

West Virginia's Loss to Pitt at Pitt

Finally, in terms of his analysis of losses, one of his earliest disappointments, while he was still coaching at West Virginia, is most informative of Coach Bowden's current style and philosophy. Unlike the explanations for the losses to Oklahoma and Florida, he took full responsibility for this defeat.

Pitt was West Virginia's biggest rival and, on this particular day in 1970, Bobby Bowden and his West Virginia team were whipping Pitt in its own back yard. The half-time score was 35-8. The final score was 36-35 in favor of Pitt. Clearly a devastating loss after such a big lead on a bitter rival.

Coach Bowden's reaction to this loss was one of profound disappointment. "It was the worst day in my life at coaching. That one killed me...that's the lowest day of my career ... even to the point of wanting to quit coaching."

When asked for his analysis of the loss he replied, "As far as the coaching is concerned, got too conservative, pulled in the reins when we got ahead of them. Just tried to win the game and not do anything ... ended up getting beat. Should have went ahead and played wide open. That's why I don't ever pull off the dogs anymore."

When asked if the loss affected his coaching philosophy, Coach Bowden replied: "I never sit on the ball anymore. Have you read the paper? They accuse me of running up the score. I never sit on the ball anymore... we attack no matter what the score is. I'm being a little facetious but it's kind of true too. I'd be playing somebody here and it's because of that game, I'm sure. We'll be ahead 40 to 19 with two minutes to go and I'm thinking all of that time, what if they scored, get an onside kick, scored, and get it again? I'm scared we could lose, you know, so I don't sit on it. A lot of people look at it and say 'You've got them beat, why do you do that? You got them beat.' But I'm still trying to score. I'm still scared. It's the results of that game."

Beating Michigan at Michigan—1991

Coach Bowden's reactions to his biggest wins also help to explain how his CR for developing a winning team has evolved over the years. One of the biggest wins was the victory over Michigan at Michigan in 1991. As he explains, "We were number one in the nation going into that game and Michigan was probably the top-ranked team on our schedule. Maybe not, I think Miami ended up higher ranked. But Michigan was a top three team, and playing them at their place, they were favored. And we beat them at their place. It was just a great accomplishment. Beat the heck out of them too. We played well."

Coach Bowden's explanation for the win was as follows: "We just executed well. Casey Weldon, Amp Lee, Marvin Jones, Terrell Buckley, all of them. We just played well as a team. Everything worked for us. We tried several trick plays and they all worked." In addition, he noted that Florida State had had an open date the week before and "that always helps." Thus, there was no single reason for the victory. It was a combination of preparation, execution, and the talent he had recruited. In addition, he notes that the win had virtually no impact on how he prepared for future games. "Usually when you're successful you just live off of that, you know. You just use that same plan. You don't change when you are successful. You change when you get beat." Thus, as the saying goes, there appears to be more lessons learned from losses than from wins. This observation is validated by CR theory and research that indicates that changes in causal patterns and causal thinking are precipitated by disappointment and unexpected outcomes rather than achievements and positive outcomes. This observation is also borne out in Coach Bowden's description of his early victory over Pitt.

Pitt at West Virginia

As described before, Pitt was West Virginia's most intense rivalry. As Coach Bowden describes this game: "It was my birthday and my son Tommy caught two or three key passes in the game. It was on national television, so that was a day when everything worked out splendidly. [We] beat them on the last play of the game. As the ball went over the goal post, the game ended. Just one of those days where you couldn't ask for a better ending if you were writing a book. It was my birthday, national television, number one rivalry, our biggest rival, and my son Tommy played for us and had two or three key catches in the game: kept drives going. [I] Had a great birthday."

In terms of his personal feeling about the game Coach Bowden said, "One of those days where you say: 'why is all of this good stuff happening to me?' You know every time Tommy would catch a pass, or we'd make a first down, or stopped them, or kicked a field goal, you'd say, boy it can't get no better than this. You know that feeling. Can't get no better than this. This is why you coach." In describing the reasons for the victory Coach Bowden explained, "We were excellently prepared and our kids were focused on the game and we played a great ball game. Our coaching staff had done a great job, especially Chuck Klausing, he was our defensive coordinator. We held Tony Dorsett to 106 yards. I remember that. We held Dorsett to 106 yards."

However, when asked how that victory influenced future preparation and game strategy Coach Bowden replied that it had little impact on future preparations or strategy. Thus, again, responses to losing may be more informative and have more of an impact on CR than responses to winning.

At the end of the interview, I asked Coach Bowden to tell me what he would say to other people who wanted to be successful. He replied, "In the first place you have to be in a program that can give you the facilities and the financial backing and resources to win. I don't care what kind of coach you are, you have to be in a place where there are resources to accomplish your goals. Got to get positive people that think you can reach your goal of a National Championship. When I first came here, my goal was to win a National Championship at Florida State University. I wasn't sure I really believed that, but I said it. I spread the word around enough that people around me thought I meant it and they performed up to that level. And we finally won one. Finally got to the big time: positive attitude has a lot to do with that." He went on to say, "I've always felt that persistence was the number one characteristic of a winner...more than any other thing...can't quit and cannot give up ... something we try to inspire in our players over and over. .. never quit ... it was exemplified in the Florida 31 to 31 tie. We were behind 31 to 3 and came up and tied it.... never quit, never quit."

In addition he said: "Practice is very important. We say ball games are won on Monday, Tuesday, Wednesday, and Thursdays...not Saturdays. You win the games the way you practice. Practice is vital."

I then mentioned a group of researchers who are studying expert performance and who contend that the only difference between experts and average performers is that the experts devote significantly more time to disciplined practice. I asked if practice, in and of itself, separated winners and losers. Coach Bowden disagreed that practice was the only factor in winning: "That's good if you have equal talent. If they've got better talent, you might work every second and still not get good enough. You've got to have talent in this business and then you have to work enough. Not so much how long you work but you have to work enough. Whatever enough is, you've got to get it."

Coach Bowden also commented on the characteristics of leadership: "The leadership has to be honest. Honesty ... and compassion. If you're honest with the kids you're working with and you have compassion for them, you're more likely to get more out of them."

Finally, although Coach Bowden did not mention it during the interview, I believe that his faith is an important factor in his winning attitude and philosophy. Coach Bowden is an active participant in the Fellowship for Christian Athletes and frequently preaches on Sundays. In the book, *The Seven Habits of Highly Effective Managers* by Steven Covey, one of those seven characteristics was a belief in and respect for a higher power. This quality seems particularly important when you work in a business that has as many twists and turns as college football. It would be difficult to accept capricious defeats and referees' decisions without a belief that there is a higher reason and purpose.

In summary, Coach Bowden's CR style is most accurately described as situationally based. He tells it like it is. One of the reasons for his popularity is that, most often, everyone else sees it the same way. The players, coaches, administration, and alumni accept what Coach Bowden says without question because of his track record of honesty and integrity. Whether he wins or loses, his objective analysis of the outcome is almost always respected and he always follows through and makes the adjustments that are needed in his game plan, coaching staff, and players.

NUMBER 11

Coach Martin is another no-nonsense guy who has established an amazing record. As of the time of this writing, in the last 21 years his baseball teams have earned the right to appear in the NCAA regional tournament every single year. His teams have won the regional tournament and gone to the College World Series 12 times since he has been at Florida State, and eight times in the last 10 years. When asked about his three most memorable successes, Coach Martin indicated that his criterion for success was whether or not the team wins the NCAA regional and the right to go to the College World Series. As he stated, "Unlike what many people believe, if we don't win the College World Series, that's not a big setback for me...I'm in it to watch expressions on young men's faces after winning a regional tournament. That to me is the greatest professional accomplishment that I as a coach have ever had. That's the high point, 'cause you start in September for that one moment to see them crying and jumping all over each other and knowing that they're going to the show. They're going where 278 schools try to get to and they're going to get there two days after the regional if we win."

Let's take a look at how Coach Martin thinks about his successful versus less successful seasons as well as some of the challenges that occurred during those campaigns.

The 1995 Regional Tournament and College World Series

As Coach Martin explained, the accomplishments of the 1995 team were "extra special for me personally because my son was the catcher and this was his second trip to the College World Series. We had two number one draft choices as pitchers and we felt like this was the year that we would win the National Championship because of the fact that we were loaded. We had every ingredient that was necessary to win it all. What a great year. We ended up 53 and 16, ranked in the top two most of the year."

When asked more specifically about the reasons why the 1995 team won the regional tournament, Coach Martin replied, "It occurred because our team felt like and expected to win. There was no doubt in anybody's mind that we were going to win. And that's so important when you have young men with positive outlooks and attitudes [internal attribution]. They took nothing for granted. There was never any lackadaisical play. It was hard-nosed baseball for nine innings. These young men appreciated the game. Some people will hit a ground ball and jog to first base and the guy throws the ball slightly high and the first baseman jumps up and catches it and comes down with his foot on the bag. If the guy is going full speed, and the first baseman jumps up in the air, the runner touches the bag while the first baseman is in the air. That can win you a ball game. Little things like that were never tolerated by that team. Somebody on that team would go up to the other person that may have loafed on one play and challenge him. And of course our coaches were always looking at intangibles that can always win games for you." Thus, Coach Martin made internal attributions to the team's ability (we were loaded), attitude, and effort (running out ground balls) as well as to the coaching staff's efforts in attending to the intangibles.

However, the attributions were not all clearly internal or external. As Coach Martin went on to explain, "Baseball games are not usually won, they're lost. Our players felt that they were not going to lose any. There were a number of times that we probably should not have won. But the other team made some mistakes late [external attribution] enabling us to revive that positive attitude [internal attribution]. We were down four runs in the top of the ninth inning on a cold night against North Carolina and went and scored five runs. The guy that was doing a number [external attribution] on us, had no-hit us two years prior to that, for the only time in my 31 years of Florida State baseball. . . . Lo and behold they took him out of the ball game [external attribution]. We scored five runs against the guy in relief."

Although Coach Martin described the 1995 season as a success, it is also instructive to look at his CR for the games that they eventually lost at the College World Series. Coach Martin explained that although the team went to the College World Series, "we endured a very tough situation in that one of our stud pitchers was hurt and wasn't able to pitch effectively." He also said, "The fact that we did not win the National Championship, I would not let it distract from a great season." Thus, Coach Martin attributed the loss to one of his key players being hurt, which suggested that the loss was not controllable. From a CR standpoint, the attribution he made appeared to be internal (i.e., hurt) but could also be interpreted as external (i.e., was hurt by some uncontrollable factor). Theory would suggest that this is a healthy attribution in that it does not place responsibility for the loss on either the coach or the team members and thus would not affect beliefs about their abilities to succeed in the future.

The 1992 Club

Of the successful 1992 club Coach Martin said, "1992 could have been a higher point for me than '94 and '95, because the 1992 club was not very good but they didn't know it and I wasn't going to tell them . . . We had a very average club. We were slow and we made up for it by being not very good hitters. After losing a series at Clemson with abusive fans, I was mad and I challenged them in a different way...We got back to Tallahassee at 12 in the morning and we went straight to the practice field and we put the lights on and we practiced. Kids left at 1:30 and met me back in the clubhouse at 6:30 in the morning. We practiced again. Now we had to take off that afternoon because of the rules. I've never done anything like that before ... I was literally at my wits end . . . I was scared . . . Where were we going? . . . I was scared and we needed to do something . . . Not very many people were happy with me when I called another 6AM practice on Tuesday and Wednesday and Thursday. On Friday we played a very average baseball team, and we lost. We lost eight to six. When I walked into that clubhouse, I was praying that I would say the right thing. It was like a morgue. Nobody was moving. Nobody looked at me. They were looking like they were expecting another a tongue lashing, or a 'see you in the morning at six o'clock.' I remember saying to them I'm sorry (I get emotional thinking about this) and I walked out. Ten minutes later everything was okay. Everything was back to normal but I couldn't talk to them because I didn't know what to say. I didn't want to degrade them, because they had played hard. That's why baseball is the greatest game in the world. Because the worst teams in the major leagues win 30 per cent of their games [notice the attribution suggests good luck]. So the next night there was no meeting. There was no tongue-lashings. It was play baseball and we ended up going back up to Clemson in the ACC tournament and we were really excited about competing against them because they had beaten us so bad. This time when we got beat I made light of it to our baseball team. The reason was we were getting ready to go into a regional tournament. That baseball team, after getting beat again, came home, lost the first game of the regional tournament one to nothing to Western Carolina, turned around and won five in a row to advance to the College World Series. And I always refer to that particular tournament as the miracle at Howser. Probably that team showed more character and determination [internal attribution] than any that I've ever had. They could have quit. They could have pointed fingers. But they literally took it on themselves to produce. I'll never forget that baseball team. We even went to the College World Series and won a game. That was better than the '91 team did and the '91 team was ranked number one most of the year. The '92 team was just a middle of the pack team. Never forget that bunch."

Barry Blackwell

Although Coach Martin initially indicated that his recent regional victories were his three most positive experiences, he also related a very positive experience with Barry Blackwell that is important for understanding the CR processes that are typical of his managerial style. As he told it, "Twelve or thirteen years ago I was a disciplinarian and I gave my players no choice. You did things the way I wanted them done. No explanation. When a player retaliated, I'd tell him 'If you don't like it, get out of here.' There was no time for discussion. As I look back, I probably alienated some players. I wasn't smart enough to realize that people have different personalities. It's still my way or the highway, but now you have an opportunity to express yourself. For example, in 1986, I started to become a leader. A lot of things happened. But I remember Barry Blackwell, who was a good catcher, coming into my office and asking to move from third base to catcher. Three years earlier I would have told him, 'If you don't like where you are, you might consider transferring.' I went on to tell him that the other catcher couldn't play another position as well and if Barry caught, we would have to put a less talented player at third base. When this was explained, I also told him that I would take care of professional scouts and we did things in batting practice to demonstrate his skills as a catcher. So during that particular explanation, 30 minutes in the office, I gained the respect of Barry. Maybe not his acceptance of the decision, but I gained his respect in that I took the time to explain it to him. He wasn't any more happy when he left the office because he didn't get what he wanted. But I didn't alienate him. He became a supporter. He became a team player. As a result of that meeting, and I'm just thankful to the good Lord that I changed [internal attribution], and became a more .....of a man. Let's put it this way. Barry Blackwell calls me to this day and says thank you for what you did for me when I was 21 years old—and he calls me on Father's Day."

The 1993 Season

The 1993 club was initially listed by Coach Martin as one of his disappointments because the team did not win the NCAA Regional Tournament. Nevertheless, as he talked of this "failure", it became clear that Coach Martin's experiences with this club helped lay the foundation for future successes. Of this club Coach Martin said: "The '93 club was not a disappointment because they were all freshmen. I was more disappointed with myself [internal attribution] in '93 because as we entered the regional tournament we were a number two seed playing in our own backyard with freshmen at first, second, and first year catching which was Mike. Freshmen pitchers, just extremely young, and I didn't have the confidence in that club that I should have [internal attribution]. I felt inwardly that we had gone just about as far as we could go. I was really disappointed with myself when that regional tournament was over because I didn't go into that regional tournament with the real positive [i.e., optimistic] outlook. And it was very unusual for me to have that, but yet I couldn't bring myself to the point that I had always brought myself to in that we're going to win this thing, we're going back to the College World Series. I saw the other clubs. I knew what the other clubs had. They were experienced [external attribution]. They were juniors and seniors. Notre Dame was very good. Long Beach State was very good. They were the number one seed. Had one of the top pitchers in the country. But when all was said and done and we had played the game and we had been eliminated, we got beat by Long Beach and then by Notre Dame. After we had won our first two I was just livid with myself. Took me two days to realize that I myself had a couple of doubts [internal attribution] and if a Seminole would have had those doubts, he would have never played. It would have showed up in his play [because he was not thinking like a winner]. And it was a lesson that was learned. I thank God that I was able to take that experience and say I will never feel this way again. Since that year, I've never had that feeling again and it's been over 125 games [excellent example of the role that causal reasoning plays in learning and adjusting management style] and as a result of that experience, I feel that I am a better preparer of young men because the team is going to feed off of me. If I felt that way inside, somebody could feel my feelings. Somebody could feel the way I felt. What made me so mad was the year before we weren't as good as we were in '93 and yet I went to the regional tournament saying, 'we're going to win this thing.' And we did. And yet in '93 with all of these young players I looked at it as a very insurmountable task [external and stable pessimistic attribution]. But I'm thankful, I'm truly thankful that I've had that experience because (He knocks on the table-knock on wood) it will not happen again. In '94 we won. In '95 we won. We accomplished our goals."

The 1995 Club

"That was a heck of a ball club. They went through the motions on the road during spring break. Jonathan Johnson who signed for 1.3 million dollars was rocked. Duke rocked him. We lost 13 to 6. Jonathan pitched hard. He always pitched hard. But we started making mistakes behind him. Duke realized we were human and the rest is history. What made it bad is we had lost a ball game before we went into Duke. That was our second loss in a row. Now we were good. We knew we were good. But we were starting to believe that we could throw our glove out there and have success. Motivation had to take place from the coaching staff. Early morning detail was formed. The guys, being as talented as they were, didn't really appreciate this. They thought they were being picked on by the extra work that they were required to do. If winning a popularity contest is high on any coach's list, he needs to change professions because my own son stopped coming to the room to go over hitters. My first baseman and team leader Doug Mientkiewicz didn't smile at me any more. This lasted for a couple of weeks. When the team started enjoying success and reeled off nine out of the next ten, things returned to normal. But I think the team realized at that point that they had to play hard [internal attribution] for 27 outs. And I as a coach realized the most important goal professionally that I have and that is I got to watch them in May."

Philosophy

During our conversation about how Coach Martin analyzed both his successes and failures, Coach Martin also commented on how his coaching philosophy changed over the years. As he stated: "Mike Martin started in 1980 with Earl Weaver's philosophy: 3-run homers. Somebody hit one out. Well, five years in a row, we would get to regional tournaments and the hitting would go south. We changed our philosophy to pitching and defense because they're more constant [stable attribution]. You don't have too many bad nights on defense. You don't have too many bad nights pitching. Why? Because if you prepared a number of pitchers, you get him out or go get somebody else. For five pitchers to have bad nights is a little unusual. But it can happen and it has happened. But anyway, that's the philosophy that we incorporate."

Luck and Chance

Coach Martin also commented on the role of luck and chance in team success. "There is more luck and chance in hitting than pitching. There is luck and chance in both of them, but there is more in hitting." To clarify this statement further, recalling an interview after a home run which won a key game in the College World Series for Florida State, I asked Coach Martin if he recalled saying that the player had been very lucky that day. He replied, "I sure do and I said it...trying to be sure I said the right thing for...the other team in case we played them later...because you might turn around and play them again. When you are speaking after an emotional win like that, you want to be careful that you don't say anything that could rile up the other bunch to make them perform at a higher level the next game [impression management]. That was the reason I used the word lucky." I then asked him what he said to the player [J.D. Drew] who hit the home run. He replied, "He was a freshman. The emotions of his teammates was all he needed. He didn't need me. I shook his hand at the end of the game and said something like 'great job' and let it go at that. He didn't need me. So the wind was blowing out to left field [external attribution]. The left-hander threw him a fastball away. He went with the pitch [internal attribution]. God has blessed him with tremendous hand speed [internal attribution], which enables him to get the bat traveling much faster than average people. I would say we just happened to have the right man at the plate with the right conditions." Thus, as you can see in this case, Coach Martin identified both internal and external causes for J.D. Drew's outstanding performance and the team victory. In addition, he commented on why we must be careful about how we interpret attributions that are made in a public setting. More will be said about the impression management aspects of public attributions in Chapter Ten.

Faith

Finally, because Coach Martin mentioned his faith several times during the interview, I asked him about the role that faith played in his successes. Coach Martin said, "I am a firm believer. The things that a person wants, he may not achieve...I prayed to make it in the big leagues...and I look back on it and I see why I didn't play in the big leagues. I wasn't mature enough at that point in my life. I may have gone in another direction. I may have messed up things if God would have answered that particular prayer. He gave me a million times more happiness and success as a result of putting me in this position right here. God put me in the position that I'm in right now. Oh sure I worked. But God gave me the opportunity to work at Florida State and then things started happening that enabled me to get the head-coaching job. And it's just been the most wonderful experience professionally that a man could ask for. This is it. I love my job... So I know that God has taken me by the hand and led me along the way. I know He has."

Thus Coach Martin has identified his faith in God as a major causal factor for his success and, as indicated earlier in this chapter, Coach Bowden also underscores the importance of faith in his professional and daily life. While it is not entirely clear how faith fits into the context of CR theory, it appears that faith can be interpreted as a belief in a stable and external cause for both successes and failures. Thus, in the case of success, faith would lessen the tendency for one to be self-serving and take total responsibility for a victory because it would be attributed, in part, to a higher power. In the case of failure, the belief that the cause, at least in part, is due to a higher purpose that is stable and external lessens the sting of personal responsibility. Thus, when people use faith as a causal factor in thinking about their successes and failures, it appears that it may have a calming influence by lessening personal responsibility (i.e., internal and stable attributions) for the high and low points in life. In addition, it is important to note that when people share a common faith (i.e., belief system), it undoubtedly reduces the amount of bias they perceive in others because of their common interpretation of the reasons for success and failure. More will be said about faith and a predictable set of ethical principles in the last chapters.

CONCLUDING COMMENTS

The opportunity to interview coaches Bowden and Martin as well as many other successful and less successful managers convinced me that the major difference between successful versus less successful individuals is their ability to objectively analyze cause and effect and then act accordingly. Thus it doesn't seem to matter whether a person manages a football team, baseball team, a pharmaceutical sales force, a framing crew, a retail store, or a group of long haul truck drivers. A key factor in success is being able to objectively identify the reasons why you and your people succeed and fail, and then to be able to address problems and take advantage of opportunities with the appropriate behavior.

Although this conclusion appears to be simple and straightforward, the process of objective analysis is not so simple. Time after time we have all observed managers, employees, spouses, parents, and friends who were unable to objectively analyze their problems. How many times have you known a person who apparently had everything going in the right direction except for one fatal blind spot? We constantly ask ourselves why people seem to sabotage themselves and fail to see the obvious flaws in their own behaviors and the behaviors of others. These blind spots and the process of overcoming the biases that cause the blind spots are the topics of the next two chapters.

KEY POINTS

1. A major difference between successful versus less successful individuals is their ability to objectively analyze cause and effect and then act accordingly.

2. When people use faith as a causal factor in thinking about their successes and failures, it appears to have a calming influence by lessening personal responsibility (i.e., internal and stable attributions) for the high and low points in life.

3. When people share a common faith (i.e., belief system), it reduces the amount of bias they perceive in others because they share a common interpretation of the reasons for success and failure.

CHAPTER IX

PERCEPTUAL BIASES THAT CLOUD CAUSAL REASONING

Over the last thirty years, researchers have studied and gained considerable understanding of the perceptual biases that cloud objective CR. The purpose of this chapter is to communicate the results of that work. However, before describing these biases, several points need to be made. First, just like CR styles, these biases are tendencies to behave in a particular way and will not appear in all situations. A second and related point is that the objective characteristics of the actual situation are the most important determinants of the attributions that people make. Said another way, when the cause of a particular success or failure is obvious to everyone, it is less likely that biases will appear. On the other hand, when a situation is ambiguous and the causes of either success or failure are unclear, biases are more likely to affect CR. Finally, it should be noted that biases occupy a two-way street. Up to this point, we have focused primarily on how CR styles affect the way people think about their own successes and failures. However, as the discussion of CR biases develops, it will become more obvious that one of the major reasons these biases are so important is that they affect our interactions with other people who are also subject to these biases. As will be demonstrated below, the biases employees have about their performance inevitably interact with their managers' biases about their performance and result in conflict. Similarly, the differences of opinion between husbands and wives regarding their successes and failures can often be traced to CR biases. Thus, virtually all complex interpersonal relationships are affected by CR biases. Finally, although we said earlier that the objective characteristics of the situation usually determine the causal analysis, it is important to realize that in any relationship, over time, ambiguous situations are inevitable and thus conflicts in perceptions about causes for both successes as well as problems are inevitable. As these conflicts continue to occur over time, they tend to exacerbate the intensity of the biases and, although the biases usually have a small impact on any single situation, over time, the biases take their toll and can result in considerable conflict and misunderstanding. The information presented below will help you recognize these biases in yourself and others, understand why they occur, how they operate, and enable you to reduce the impact of these biases on your own CR processes and interpersonal relationships.

THE SELF-SERVING BIAS

The self-serving bias is the tendency to take credit for success (internal attribution) and blame others for failure (external attribution). Research has demonstrated that the self-serving bias is a natural tendency. Most people have a tendency to take credit for success and blame something or someone else for their failures even though they think they are objective. We are all familiar with this bias. Almost everyone has experienced leaders and co-workers who take inappropriate credit for group and organizational successes. Similarly, almost everyone has experienced the outrage that occurs when someone who is clearly responsible for a very visible failure tries to tag the blame on someone or something else. If we are totally honest with ourselves, we can probably remember at least one incident where we took credit for something we didn't do. You may also be able to recall a situation where you blamed a problem you created on something or someone else.

There are several explanations for this bias. The first is that the self-serving bias protects our self-esteem. We all want to feel good about ourselves and we all try to avoid threats to our self-esteem. Taking credit for success helps us feel good about ourselves. Blaming something or someone else for our problems protects us from feeling bad about ourselves, at least in the short run.

Another plausible explanation is the need to create a positive impression of oneself. This explanation suggests that the need to be perceived positively by others motivates us to take credit for success and blame others when failures occur.

Finally, we can explain this bias as a form of hedonism. In general, we all want to receive rewards and avoid punishment. This bias appears to maximize rewards while minimizing punishment.

Numerous studies have been conducted which document the existence and effects of the self-serving bias. The research shows that the bias is pervasive and affects many aspects of CR that affect intrapersonal and interpersonal behavior. Most people exhibit this bias to some degree.

THE ACTOR-OBSERVER BIAS

The actor-observer bias is the pervasive tendency of observers to attribute the successes and failures of the actor (i.e., the person being observed) to internal characteristics (e.g., ability) as opposed to the actor's tendency to attribute the same outcomes to external situational circumstances (i.e., an external attribution). At the time this is being written (September, 1998) Mark McGwire and Sammy Sosa (the actors) have both hit 66 home runs. When news reporters and the average fan (i.e., the observers) explain why these two athletes are doing so well, they constantly refer to the attributes of the athletes such as quick wrists, fast reactions, keen eyesight, and physical strength. On the other hand, when asked to account for their success after hitting a home run, the athletes focus on the situation rather than their personal characteristics. For example, Mark McGwire has repeatedly said that when the pitchers give him a ball he can drive, he can hit it out of the park. On the other hand, in interviews after games when he has not hit a home run, he has repeatedly stated that it is a situation he cannot control and whether or not and when he hits another home run depends on whether or not the pitcher gives him a ball he can drive (external attribution). Similarly, if you ask a real estate agent about a successful sale, an investment banker after a successful public offering, or a plant manager about a good year, each one is likely to attribute success (or failure) to the situation and circumstances surrounding the performance environment. The real estate agent will talk about the "perfect match" between the buyer and the property, the investment banker will emphasize the timing and viability of the offering, and the plant manager will probably refer to factors such as a good labor environment and growing economy. On the other hand, as outsiders (observers), we tend to attribute the success or failure of the real estate agent, investment banker, and plant manager to their own personal characteristics.

Why does the actor-observer bias occur? The consensus of both research and theory is that, during the performance, the focus of the performer's (actor's) attention is on the performance environment (i.e., the pitcher). On the other hand, the focus of the observer's attention is on the actor. Thus, for example, the fans (observers) are watching Mark McGwire but Mark McGwire (the actor) is watching the pitcher. Thus, when we ask either party to explain Mark McGwire's success, we get two very different explanations based on where their attentions were focused. Mark McGwire's explanation emphasizes what he was attending to at the time of the performance—the pitcher. On the other hand, the fans explain McGwire's performance in terms of the focus of their attention—Mark McGwire. Thus actors and observers literally see things differently because they are paying attention to different things.

The implications of the actor-observer bias are profound. They help us understand why two people can have an entirely different perception of what happened when they appear to be seeing the exact same thing. The actor-observer bias makes it clear that they are really not seeing the same thing. The actor's primary attention is on the environment surrounding his or her behavior whereas the observer is focusing on the actor. Again, it is important to note that like other biases, the actor-observer bias is a tendency. It does not mean that observers are totally unaware of the environment or that actors are not aware of the importance of their efforts and abilities. It does mean however, that the scale tips toward situational explanations by the actor and internal dispositional explanations for the actor's behavior by observers. This slight amount of bias may not make a great deal of difference when the causes of success or failure are clear or when the actor and observer are not involved in a long-term relationship where both parties depend on one another. On the other hand, it can often be a primary source of conflict in long-term relationships such as between employers and employees, husbands and wives, and parents and children, because, over time, the biases will come into play and perceptions of important situations will inevitably differ.

FALSE CONSENSUS EFFECT

This bias is the result of observers believing that their own behaviors and choices are typical and appropriate and then using them as a standard by which to judge the behavior and performance of others. Thus, observers often assume that they are "average" (false consensus) and any choice beyond the one that they would make is seen as inappropriate and deviant. As a result, behavior and outcomes that conform to these self-based standards are usually attributed to the situation because observers think that this is the same way that they or anyone else would react to the same situation. On the other hand, behavior that is unusual and believed to be atypical is attributed to the internal characteristics and dispositions of the actor.

Although less research has been done to confirm this bias than the others, we can all certainly recall managers, supervisors, and teachers who appeared to think that everyone should behave like them. Thus, while it would be preferable to have had more research to support this proposed bias, our experience suggests that the bias would be confirmed if the additional research was conducted.

HEDONIC RELEVANCE

Hedonic relevance is the notion of personal benefit. This bias suggests that to the extent that observers or actors experience personal benefit or harm as a result of the outcomes they are evaluating, their attributions for the outcomes will be biased toward optimizing their benefits. Thus, leaders are much more likely to blame subordinates (i.e., make internal attributions) when they encounter serious as opposed to minor problems. For example, if a nurse administers the wrong dosage of a prescription to a patient and the patient does not have an adverse reaction, the nursing supervisor is less likely to blame the nurse (i.e., make an internal attribution) than if the patient had an adverse reaction which could potentially result in a lawsuit. Similarly, a nurse is more likely accept blame (internal attribution) when a problem results in a minor consequence as opposed to a problem for which the consequences are serious. Thus the nature and severity of the consequences for both failure as well as success can influence the CR process.

THE EFFECT OF CR BIASES ON INTERPERSONAL RELATIONS

The discussion above makes it clear that CR biases often result in conflicting perceptions between actors and observers. Although each bias tips the scale slightly, the combined effects of the biases are often quite substantial, particularly under conditions of failure or potential failure. For example, imagine that a partner in a law firm, let's call her Mary, takes on the responsibility of contracting for a new law office for the firm. Also imagine that the firm is up and coming with numerous successful lawyers who have not yet gained the prestige necessary to command the fees and attract the cases that they would like. Thus, the task of designing and constructing the new building for the firm would have high hedonic relevance for the partners because they all want a prestigious office in a prestigious firm. Yet, because they are not yet doing as well as they would like, the bottom line cost of the building also has high hedonic relevance. Moreover, because they are all busy, they are hesitant to become involved in the day-to-day planning and construction of the office.

Assume now that Mary, sensing that they do not want to become involved in the day-to-day planning, accepts the responsibility for the new office, receives a very general commitment on a budget, and a set of guidelines at the monthly partners' meeting. She then forges ahead with the plans (she also has her own clients to attend to), hires an architect, lets out a bid informing her partners of her actions, accepts the bid, is in the last stage of finalizing the contract with the contractor, and must now have her partners sign off on the contract. At this point, the rubber meets the road and all hell breaks loose as the partners start examining the details of the architectural plan and contract (they are all lawyers, so they know everything about contracts). Several partners accuse Mary of slighting them because the square footage of their offices is less than that of some of the other partners. Others are unhappy that, although they have more square footage in their offices than others, they have been allocated interior offices without windows. Some are appalled at the estimated cost, exclaiming that it is fifty dollars per square foot more than it should be. Others accuse Mary of tripping over dollars to save pennies and believe that the plans are far too modest. Mary is upset and frustrated. She has spent considerable time and effort putting the package together and has talked, at least in general terms, to everyone, telling them that she was making every effort to balance their needs with the general budget guidelines that they had agreed upon. At each step in the process they encouraged her to go forward without formal and time-consuming meetings, expressing confidence in her judgment. Furthermore, the partners are upset because, although the contract has not been finalized, the bid was accepted. Backing out now would be an embarrassment for the firm. At this point, Mary feels like her partners believe she is an idiot. Some of her partners would not disagree.

What has happened in this case is that all of the biases have converged to blame an unpleasant problem on Mary. More specifically, from the perspective of the self-serving bias (the tendency to blame failure on an external cause), the partners all have a tendency to attribute the failure to finalize the contract to Mary, saying that the failure is due to Mary's "lack of sensitivity to the needs and resources of the partners." Similarly, the actor-observer perspective tips the partners' perceptions toward blaming the failure on the internal attributes of Mary who is the focus of their attention because, in this case, she is the actor. Third, the false consensus effect takes hold and each of the partners evaluates Mary's "failure" according to his or her own set of standards, concluding that because they would have acted differently, the failure to gain consensus on the contract is Mary's fault (internal attribution). Finally, because the issue is important it has significant hedonic relevance and even though the partners should have expressed their concerns earlier and provided Mary with their input, they tend to place the blame on Mary rather than themselves. Thus, all four biases that affect observers (self-serving, actor-observer, false consensus, and hedonic relevance) generally work together in the case of failure.

Table 9-1 shows how the various observer biases converge under conditions of failure. As you can see, all of the biases work in the same direction, toward observers (leaders)

TABLE 9-1. Observer (Leader) Attributions for Actor (Member) Performance

	FAILURE	SUCCESS
SELF-SERVING	INTERNAL	EXTERNAL
ACTOR-OBSERVER	INTERNAL	INTERNAL
HEDONIC BIAS	INTERNAL	EXTERNAL
FALSE CONSENSUS EFFECT	INTERNAL	EXTERNAL

attributing the failure of actors (members) to the internal characteristics of the actor (member). To further compound the situation, Table 9-2 demonstrates that all of the actor (member) biases converge so that actors are strongly biased towards attributing their failures to external causes (which are sometimes the observer or the leader). Thus, under conditions of actor (member) failure, all of the observer (leader) biases work in the direction of blaming the actor (member) whereas the actor (member) biases all work in the direction of blaming some external cause such as a difficult task, a supervisor, co-worker, or the organization. Thus, it was not surprising when the news media appeared to blame Greg Norman for his poor showing in the last round of the 1996 Masters whereas Greg Norman appeared to contextualize it saying that he had just had a bad day at a bad time. Similarly, it was not surprising that the public and news media appeared to attribute much more culpability to President Clinton's escapades with Monica Lewinsky than the President appeared willing to acknowledge. It is possible that both observers and actors "honestly" believe that they perceive the truth but also that, as a result of their biases, they actually see a different truth.

As illustrated in both Tables 9-1 and 9-2, the effect of biases on perceptions of success is not as profound. For both the actor and the observer, several of the biases counteract each other. Thus, although the self-serving bias suggests that actors will take credit for success (internal attribution), the actor-observer bias suggests that actors will attribute their success to external environmental factors on which their

TABLE 9-2. Actors' (Members') Attributions for Their Own Performances

	FAILURES	SUCCESSES
SELF SERVING	EXTERNAL	INTERNAL
ACTOR-OBSERVER	EXTERNAL	EXTERNAL
HEDONIC BIAS	EXTERNAL	INTERNAL
FALSE CONSENSUS EFFECT	EXTERNAL	INTERNAL

attention is focused. Thus, these same two biases appear to cancel each other out in the case of actor successes. In conclusion, because the various CR biases tend to counteract one another under conditions of success, both observers (leaders) and actors (members) are probably more objective in accounting for actor (member) successes than actor (member) failures.

THE EFFECT OF CR BIASES ON THE SELF AND SELF-MOTIVATION

In addition to affecting interpersonal relations, the biases described above also affect how we think about ourselves. Moreover, they are embedded within the CR styles we discussed in earlier chapters. Thus, for example, a person with an optimistic CR style is really a person with an accentuated self-serving bias. On the other hand, pessimists have a style that is exactly the opposite of the self-serving bias. Thus, CR styles are really a shorthand way of summarizing the types of biases that people tend to demonstrate in their CR processes. Since we have already discussed how CR styles affect intrapersonal motivation, another description of how the dimensions of attributions affect motivation would be redundant. Nevertheless, recalling a couple of points regarding how the dimensional properties of these biases affect motivation will be helpful. First, as described in earlier chapters, internal attributions for success tend to enhance self-esteem and motivation whereas internal attributions for failure tend to be debilitating, potentially leading to depression and helplessness. Second, stable attributions for either success or failure increase the expectancy that the individual will have the same type of outcome in the future. Unstable attributions suggest that the outcome may change and are motivational in the face of failure but demotivational in the case of success. Thus, once again, it is emphasized that how people analyze the causes of their success and failures has a whole lot to do with how they feel about themselves and how they behave in the future.

DEFINITIONS

1. *Biases*—tendencies to think (i.e., make attributions) and behave in a particular way.

2. *Self-serving bias*—the tendency to take credit for success (internal attribution) and blame others for failure (external attribution).

3. *Actor-observer bias*—the tendency of observers to attribute the successes and failures of the actor (i.e., the person being observed) to internal characteristics (e.g., ability) as opposed to the actor's tendency to attribute the same outcomes to external situational circumstances (i.e., an external attribution).

4. *False consensus effect*—the result of observers believing that their own behaviors and choices are typical and appropriate and then using them as a standard by which to judge the behavior and performance of others.

5. *Hedonic relevance bias*—the notion that people are biased toward optimizing their personal benefits.

KEY POINTS

1. Regardless of biases, the objective characteristics of the actual situation are the most important determinants of the attributions that people make at any given moment.

2. Although biases usually have a small impact on any single situation, over time, the biases take their toll and often result in considerable conflict and misunderstanding.

3. Actors and observers literally see things differently because they are paying attention to different things.

4. Under conditions of actor (member) failure, all of the observer (leader) biases work in the direction of blaming the actor (member) whereas the actor (member) biases all work in the direction of blaming some external cause (e.g., the leader).

5. Because the various CR biases tend to counteract one another under conditions of success, both observers (leaders) and actors (members) are probably more objective in accounting for actor (member) successes than actor (member) failures.

6. The way that people analyze the causes of their success and failures has a whole lot to do with how they feel about themselves and how they behave in the future.

CHAPTER X

TOWARD AN EMOTIONALLY INTELLIGENT CR STYLE
OVERCOMING THE EFFECTS OF CR BIASES

In this chapter, methods for overcoming CR biases are presented. These methods range from very simple and straightforward suggestions such as removing ambiguity to much more intensive therapeutic processes, such as attributional retraining. Regardless of the nature and depth of these suggestions, all are directed toward enabling more objective and emotionally intelligent CR processes with the underlying tenet that, in the long run, individuals will become more empowered, enabling them to feel better about themselves and behave in much more productive ways. While methods for overcoming intrapersonal biases are stressed, this section also describes strategies for overcoming the negative affects of observer biases.

REMOVING AMBIGUITY

As suggested in Chapter Eight, one of the main triggers of biases in CR processes, and for any perceptual process, is ambiguity. CR biases can be reduced by removing ambiguity. A good example of a performance environment with minimal ambiguity is football. The objective in football is clear: to outscore the opponent. There is a clear set of rules and the referees enforce the rules. Ironically, even though the rules and game are relatively unambiguous, most of the conflicts in football are over the few aspects of the game that have some ambiguity. As a result, there are constant efforts to remove the ambiguity through tactics such as instant replay and better officiating. Nevertheless, compared to other organizations, football teams have relatively low ambiguity. In almost all programs at the college level and above, performances are graded objectively by scoring films. Statistics are kept on quarterbacks, receivers, defensive linemen (tackles and sacks) and offensive lineman (blocking percentages). As a result, coaches can be much more objective and provide their players with "less biased" feedback.

In contrast, many organizations do not have clearly defined goals, roles, or standards for performance. Performance is not graded objectively and there are environmental factors that affect performance that cannot be seen on film. While it is not being suggested that organizations, families, or personal relationships should be structured like football teams, it is suggested that clarifying objectives, roles, evaluation procedures, and performance standards is one way of minimizing ambiguity and reducing bias. Organizations often spend too little time defining strategic objectives, setting goals, negotiating roles, and clarifying performance expectations and standards. Since there are many excellent books and articles that describe how to perform these functions, the nuts and bolts are not addressed here. Hopefully, what this discussion provides is a solid rationale that makes clear why these activities are so important.

Finally, it should be noted that even if we could remove all ambiguity from our performance environments, bias would still appear because it is part of the human condition and there are many other factors that cause biases besides ambiguity. Nevertheless, when ambiguity is present, it provides fertile ground for biases to flourish. Removing ambiguity makes it less likely that biases will grow. Nonetheless, weeds appear in even the most well tended gardens and, when they do appear, these weeds are even more obvious. The reason why some football coaches are so vilified is that their biases are so much more visible against a backdrop of objective performance information. In addition, it should be noted that another reason why biases are so apparent in the arena of football is that winning and losing has high hedonic relevance. In the next section, we will address reducing bias by managing hedonic relevance.

HEDONIC RELEVANCE

The term hedonic relevance stems from the notion of hedonism: the notion that people strive to maximize their rewards and minimize their pain. Hedonists live for the moment and try to maximize their rewards. Hedonic relevance is concerned with the perceived importance of an immediate outcome. A steak dinner has high hedonic relevance for someone who likes steak and is hungry but low hedonic relevance for someone who is not hungry and doesn't like steak. The degree to which a person is likely to exhibit biases in making attributions about the causes of an outcome is proportional to the hedonic relevance (i.e., perceived importance) of the outcome. A rabid football fan who likens winning and losing to life and death is much more motivated to distort reality (i.e., perceptions and CR) than an objective observer who favors neither team.

Clearly one way of reducing CR biases is to reframe the hedonic relevance of an outcome. A good example of advice on reframing hedonic relevance is contained in Fisher and Ury's book entitled *Getting to Yes*, which is probably the best and most-read book on the art of negotiating. Much of their advice has to do with reframing people's perceptions of negotiating from a win/lose process to a win/win process. By eliminating the threat of losing and reframing the negotiation situation as one where both parties can win, the threats of face-saving losses that have high hedonic relevance are eliminated. Moreover, as the prior chapter suggested, CR biases are less likely to manifest themselves under conditions of success (win/win) as opposed to failure (win/lose or lose/lose). Thus, reframing negotiations from a win/lose to a win/win perspective helps both parties to approach the process more objectively and with less bias.

The same advice that applies to negotiating also applies to other situations that have hedonic relevance. Reframing and putting the situation into perspective decreases biases and encourages objective information processing. An example is a rabid Nebraska football fan I met some time ago who literally had a heart attack during a football game. Part of his treatment program included counseling and, at least initially, he had to refrain from attending any more Nebraska games. While I do not know what eventually happened to him, it appears safe to say that the objective of his counseling was reframing and putting into perspective the importance of winning or losing a football game as contrasted with living so that he could be more objective and less emotional (i.e., biased) when he went to a football game.

While most of us do not encounter life and death situations on a daily basis, there are a number of people who approach even minor events as life or death experiences. Comparing the importance of these minor outcomes to more important outcomes such as literally living or dying helps to put these situations in perspective and leads to less biases in the CR process.

A wide variety of experiences can help put things in perspective including the death of someone close, a serious illness, or an account of such events on TV or in literature. In addition, coaches, teachers, parents, and managers can help their players, pupils, children, and employees put things in perspective through well-timed humor, structured experiences (e.g., visiting a sick friend or reviewing a fatal accident on the job), and heart-to-heart talks.

Another suggestion for managing the biases created by hedonic relevance is to be aware of situations that are likely to have high hedonic relevance. Money has high hedonic relevance for most people and one can expect biases to enter into financial transactions. Banks, real estate agencies, and other organizations try to remove the bias and ambiguity surrounding financial transactions by formalized mortgages and closings. Similar processes and ceremonies often surround other situations where the outcomes have high hedonic relevance such as hiring, firing, marriages, divorces, promotions, and graduations. Thus, if one anticipates a situation with high hedonic relevance, one should consider traditional procedures or create procedures to formalize events so that they can be as objective and unbiased as possible.

DEVELOPING EMPATHY

A third strategy for reducing bias in interpersonal and organizational relationships is to develop empathy. Empathy is identifying with and experiencing the emotions of the other person. The easiest way to develop empathy is to put yourself in the other person's place. The actor-observer bias exists because of the different perspectives of the two parties. This knowledge suggests that literally putting yourself in the other person's shoes will reduce this bias.

There are many ways to "put yourself in another person's shoes." Senior-level Japanese managers are noted for spending at least one day a month working an entry-level job. Certainly this technique helps them see problems through the eyes of their employees. The management literature on leader/member relations documents that satisfying leader/member relations are a function of the degree to which the leaders and members feel a psychological closeness with each other. These feelings of closeness are often a function of working together in close physical proximity and of having had the same job before the leaders were promoted to managerial positions. Spouses can switch roles and jobs for a day or simply listen to each other and assure one another that they have heard what the other party is saying.

There are many sources that describe how to develop empathetic and caring relations. Hopefully, the understanding provided here as to how empathy works to reduce biases and engender more productive and fruitful relationships will provide the motivation and rationale for consulting these sources.

INCREASING PHYSICAL PROXIMITY AND INTERACTION

Closely related to the concept of developing empathy is the notion that increasing physical and psychological closeness reduces biases. In the same set of studies referred to above, it was found that physical and psychological proximity are often associated with positive leader and member relations. An example of the application of the principle of reducing bias through physical proximity is the process of assigning offices at Florida State's School of Business. Although the business school, like many businesses, is divided into functional areas (e.g., marketing, accounting, finance, and management), one of our first deans believed it was dysfunctional to assign offices by department. The current process for assigning offices intermingles professors from all of the functional areas so that individual professors are as likely to be across the hall from someone from another department as someone from their own department. Because the development of personal relations is often facilitated by physical proximity, many friendships between people from different departments are encouraged because of the physical arrangement of the offices. As a result, friendly acts and information are exchanged between members of different departments who would not otherwise have a reason to interact. Thus, at least some of the biases between members of different departments are minimized because of familiarity.

There are many other examples of situations that appear to be structured to benefit from the notion that increased interaction and physical proximity encourages teamwork (thereby reducing biases). Examples include annual sales meetings, business entertainment, lobbying, and team-building programs which structure challenging outdoor activities. Although outsiders may sometimes question these types of activities, the time, effort, and expense devoted to these programs makes it clear that senior level managers believe that there is considerable benefit resulting from these programs.

A complete description of the process of developing structured experiences is beyond the scope of this book. References for sources that might be helpful in designing structured experiences are provided in the notes for this chapter at the end of the book. Hopefully, the explanation provided above provides a useful foundation for deciding whether or not increasing proximity or engaging in structured activities will be helpful.

IMPRESSION MANAGEMENT

The study of impression management is a relatively new area of organizational research and demonstrates that impression management can be a powerful method of reducing the effects of biases. This research demonstrates that people can successfully and purposely manipulate information and their self-images to create desired impressions. With respect to attributional biases, the impression management strategies of accounts, apologies, and information manipulation have been demonstrated to affect the attributions that leaders make for member behaviors. In general, when members provide an account that refers to factors that reduce the member's responsibility for poor performance, leaders are more lenient in their disciplinary actions. Similarly, when individuals apologize for a transgression and acknowledge that the behavior was inappropriate and not intended to cause harm, the recipient of the wrongdoing is less likely to make an internal and stable attribution for the transgression. Finally, manipulating information to demonstrate mitigating circumstances can reduce the probability that an observer (e.g., leader or manager) will hold another person responsible (i.e., make an internal and stable attribution) for poor performance. Thus, accounts, apologies, and information manipulation can all serve to reduce observer biases.

These types of strategies must be used with caution and integrity. There is evidence that these strategies can backfire when they are seen as manipulative and insincere. However, the balance of the research demonstrates that accounts, apologies, and information manipulation can be very successful strategies in avoiding the negative impressions caused by attributions of responsibility (i.e., internal and stable) when the impression management attempts are seen as genuine and sincere.

MULTIPLE RATERS

Another strategy that can help reduce bias is the use of multiple raters. Different raters will have different levels of experience with the performances being rated, the person being rated, and differences in the hedonic relevance of the performances. The differences in their perspectives will cause some differences of opinion regarding the attributions for a person's performance. Moreover, confronting these differences in perspectives is likely to influence the raters to think about the factors that may have caused the differences, thereby encouraging CR processes to be more explicit and systematic. This effort to be more systematic should result in less bias in the attributions that are eventually made for performance.

ATTRIBUTIONAL RETRAINING

Attributional retraining is aimed at changing your CR style or the CR style of another person so that the CR is a source of empowerment for both the individual and others. The change process can be facilitated through a therapist but it can also be effectuated through self-study, examination, and feedback. This book, the self-tests, and the sources quoted at the end of the book can all help serve as a guide.

The objective of attributional retraining depends very much on the current CR style of the target person. Individuals who tend to make internal attributions for failure and external attributions for success such as the Accommodators, Pluggers, Pessimists, and Tragedians will probably want to move more toward internal and stable attributions for success and external and unstable attributions for failure. On the other hand, people with accentuated self-serving biases who are extremely optimistic may want to move toward more objective analyses of their failures as well as their successes.

How do you change? As suggested above, self-analysis and self-talk is a start. Feedback from an objective third party can also be helpful. Also, comparative information about other people and comparisons of your present performance with your past performance over time can be helpful. To demonstrate how this works, I will use a personal example. About four years ago, I decided that I would take up golf more seriously. I had been a caddie when I was 13 and 14 years old but had only played once or twice a year since then. Like everyone, after I decided to become more serious, I wanted to be good. But I didn't always play as I would like. At times, when I would hit a bad shot, I would become irritated with myself and said things, at least subliminally, like "you idiot, you can't do anything right." Fortunately, I made the connection between my professional life and my recreation and began a thorough analysis of my CR style as it related to golf (incidentally, there is evidence that people may have different CR styles for different behavioral domains. Thus a person may be pessimistic about success at golf but optimistic about the potential of career success). Part of my CR analysis involved realizing that I was not alone. I observed countless other golfers beating themselves up over their games. From this I could conclude "it's not only me, but other people also become frustrated because golf is a very difficult game (external attribution)." Another part of my analysis involved comparing my current performance with past performances. When I did this I could see that I had shot a number of rounds in the seventies but that, occasionally, I also pushed the century mark. There was no particular pattern and exceptionally good rounds (and shots) could follow exceptionally bad rounds (and shots) and vice versa. Thus I had to conclude that my poor performances were not inevitable (i.e., they were unstable) and that, at times, I demonstrated the ability to play well. Finally, part of my "therapy" involved going to two golf professionals (my analysts) and getting my swing evaluated. Both indicated that I had a sound swing, good grip, and substantial power. Thus I was able to conclude that I had the ability (internal attribution) to score well and, as importantly, my poor scoring was not due to a lack of innate ability. In addition, one of pros also asked me a very good question: "What is your ~~ob~~jective?" After some discussion with her, it became clear to ~~m~~e that I could shoot in the low seventies and potentially even do better, but it would probably require at least six months and at least two hours of practice about four times a week. That discussion rang my bell and woke me up. My self-talk now is something to the effect of "you have the ability to be an excellent golfer if you practice hard. If you don't practice and play poorly, the reason is a lack of practice (internal/unstable effort) rather than a lack of ability (internal /stable). You can gradually improve your game with more experience and practice. But you can never optimize it until you make a commitment and practice the way you need to." At that point, I realized that I did not want to make that kind of commitment to golf and that my goal was to get some exercise (I prefer to walk) and to enjoy a reasonable round of golf. Now when I hit a bad shot, I rarely become angry. My self-talk is something to the effect of "that wasn't very good but you haven't practiced enough to expect to do better on a consistent basis. But, since you have the ability, if you continue to concentrate, the next shot can be much better." Now I keep my concentration, enjoy my game, play each shot one at a time, and try to optimize my performance while I'm on the course. I've made a conscious decision that I don't want to pay the price (at least now) of reducing my handicap, so I can't expect to always play well.

We can also use the golf example to illustrate how we can use our knowledge of CR styles to help others. One of my favorite quotes is from Jack Nicklaus who was asked what the biggest weaknesses were in the average golfer's game. His reply was that their expectations are too high. Said another way, there are many golfers out there with healthy Mr. or Ms. Responsible CR biases who believe that success and failure in golf is a function of their ability, which is only partly true. When they play well, they get all puffed up and cocky because they believe that it is the result of their superior ability. On the other hand, and more often, when they play poorly, they get all puffed up and sore at themselves, throw clubs, and generally abuse themselves and others around them because they feel so bad about themselves.

Admittedly, there is little another person can do unless the partner asks for help. But when they do, what do you say? Again, it depends on what their biases are, but for most golfers it makes sense to say something to the effect of "You certainly have the ability to play well, but, to put things in perspective, the pros spend several hours a day practicing. Unless you (and I) put in that kind of time practicing, we really can't expect to play well on a consistent basis." More to the point, I have a young son who is sometimes amenable to coaching. My constant theme to him is that he has the ability but that he has to practice in order to play well. Occasionally he will say that he is no good (internal and stable-pessimistic). At that point I step in, reassure him that he is already playing much better than other kids his age (comparative information), he has a great swing and awesome power (his ability is excellent), that he has hit great shots in the past (comparing present performance with past performance), but that he has just not practiced enough (effort) to consistently hit excellent shots. I also remind him that Tiger Woods constantly played and practiced from a very early age. Finally, I am careful to let him know that he doesn't have to spend his time playing golf, but that if he decides that he wants to play and be good at it, the only road to success will be through practice.

The same principles apply to almost all areas of human achievement. However, this is not a ten-step cookbook for success. The exact words that you as a leader, coach, parent, or manager say to empower high performance depends on the person's CR in that specific situation and your knowledge of that situation. Most of the time the theme is that "you have the ability to be successful if you apply constant effort (i.e., practice) over a period of time." However, this approach is not always on target. Occasionally, someone does not have the ability to succeed at a particular type of endeavor, contradicting the myth that all people are created equal in talent. In such cases, a thorough analysis of the causal properties of the situation is needed. For example, one of the most serious students I ever had was unable to succeed in graduate school. He came to me looking for help after he did poorly in my class as well as in several others. Together we did a thorough analysis of his study habits, the amount of time he spent studying, and the success he had achieved. We found that, compared to other students, he spent about two to three times more time studying and took excellent notes in class. However, in our discussions, it became clear that he memorized most of the material but was unable to integrate the concepts. He had done well as an undergraduate because many of the exams required only rote memorization. He also admitted that, as an undergraduate, he had difficulty with integrative subjects such as English, and his wife helped him write most of his term papers, even though he still spent far more time on them than the average student. Finally, we checked his college and graduate admission test scores and found that they were well below average. He then admitted that he had always tested low on IQ tests and general knowledge tests. However, he almost always tested well on specific subjects in high school and as an undergraduate because he worked extremely hard and memorized the material. Thus it was not test anxiety, because he performed well on some tests but poorly on others. He eventually concluded that he did not have the type of ability that would result in a productive research or academic career. On the other hand, when we examined his strengths, which included high energy, excellent interpersonal skills, and an incredible memory, we concluded that his assets would enable him to succeed well in the business world. Eventually, he took a job in sales. Today, he is well past a six-figure income and has a rich and full life, enjoying both his business and family relationships. He calls me about twice a year and considers me one of his mentors even though it was my course that "flunked" him out of the program.

Before leaving this section, there are a couple of important points that need to be clarified. The examples described above often referred to comparisons with other people and the consistency of behavior over time. Comparisons with other people are one of the primary sources of information that we use to determine whether or not success and failure are due to internal or external causes. For example, if during a ball game everyone in the line-up gets a hit off an opposing pitcher, the players, coaches, and observers will usually attribute the hits to poor pitching (i.e., an external situational cause), since everyone got a hit. On the other hand, if a pitcher throws a three-hitter and the same batter gets all three hits, the three hits will usually be attributed to the ability of the batter (internal attribution). Thus, in general, when everyone performs alike, we tend to attribute the performance to the situation. When a person's performance stands out compared to that of other people in the same situation, we tend to attribute the performance to the internal characteristics of the person. From a coaching perspective, this same type of information can influence CR style. Letting someone know that other people have the same problems allows the person to conclude that the cause of the problem is external as opposed to internal. Oftentimes, especially with inexperienced employees and young people, a manager, mentor, or coach can be extremely helpful explaining that he or she or others also have or have had the same difficulties. Such feedback enables people to make external attributions and avoid feeling inadequate and becoming depressed about themselves.

Comparing a current performance with past performances over time in the same types of situations provides the information that is needed to determine whether or not a cause is stable or unstable. For example, if a customer relations representative gets good reviews from customers and has always received positive reviews from customers, the performance will usually be attributed to a stable cause such as ability. However, assume that this customer relations representative has an Accommodator CR style, and tends to attribute problems to what she perceives to be her own internal and stable lack of ability. Furthermore, suppose this person runs into a particularly irate customer who then files a discrimination lawsuit against the company, naming and blaming this representative. Then, because of the tendency to blame herself for problems, this representative begins to believe that she caused a problem that could have been avoided. This is problematic for two reasons. First, if called to testify, the employee may admit some wrongdoing when, in fact, there was none. Second, and more importantly, from a humanistic perspective, the employee may become depressed, blame herself, and no longer function effectively on the job. A manager or supervisor can help this person overcome the feelings of poor self-esteem that result from approaching a problem in this frame of mind by stressing the employee's record of consistent excellent performance over time and stressing that the employee's ability is the most likely cause of such consistent high performance in the past. Moreover, convincing the person that the cause of the current problem is not lack of ability may also help the representative understand that the cause was an unstable isolated incident (i.e., a weird customer), and something for which she should not assume responsibility. Thus, based on stable past performance, poor performance is not expected to occur again in the future. Thus, consistency information is a primary tool for demonstrating that causes are stable or unstable, enabling individuals to be more hopeful about their expectations of future successes.

In conclusion, attribution retraining is aimed at empowering oneself and empowering other people by replacing biased CR with emotionally intelligent CR that fosters self-esteem and facilitates reasonable expectations for success in the future. In general, dysfunctional CR: (a) reduces expectations for success or encourages unrealistic expectations for success and (b) attacks self-esteem or builds unrealistic self-esteem. The exact nature of the changes in CR depends upon the CR that is currently dominating one's thinking. Thus, people with overly optimistic styles may need to confront their own culpability for their failures whereas overly pessimistic people will generally need to move toward appreciating their own potential to succeed. At the risk of being oversimplistic, a summary of suggestions for overcoming biased CR and adopting empowered CR processes is provided in Table 10-1.

A discussion of each of the steps in Table 10-1 is embedded in the previous material. However, several aspects of the process deserve additional comment. First, it is important to start the change process with an objective assessment of a person's CR for a specific performance. Beginning with nebulous things such as changing a "poor attitude" doesn't work because the goal of the change process will not be clear.

Thus, just as in any other type of behavior change process, beginning with an identifiable and objective assessment of performance starts the process off on solid ground. In some cases, especially when the individual initiates the change process, this first step may be aided by a more formalized assessment of CR style with a standardized instrument such as the self-test provided in the second chapter of the book. Additional measures of CR style are listed in the references for Chapter Two at the end of the book.

The second step, comparing current with past performance helps to determine whether or not the causes of a performance problem are stable or unstable. The baseball example, the test performance problem, and the irate customer example all illustrated how comparing past with present performances can help determine the stability of a

TABLE 10-1. FIVE STEPS TOWARD EMPOWERED CR

1. IDENTIFY CURRENT CR REGARDING AN IMPORTANT AND SPECIFIC PERFORMANCE
2. COMPARE CURRENT PERFORMANCE WITH PAST PERFORMANCE (I.E., ASSESS STABILITY)
3. COMPARE CURRENT AND PAST PERFORMANCES WITH THOSE OF RELEVANT OTHERS (I.E., ASSESS INTERNAL/EXTERNAL DIMENSIONS)
4. CONSIDER THE ABOVE INFORMATION ALONG WITH CR STYLE, AND ARRIVE AT A REALISTIC ATTRIBUTION FOR THE CAUSES OF THE SPECIFIC PERFORMANCE (feedback and discussion with an objective third party may be particularly helpful at this point)
5. BASED ON WHETHER THE CAUSE IS INTERNAL OR EXTERNAL AND STABLE OR UNSTABLE, DEVELOP AN ACTION PLAN THAT EMPOWERS SUCCESS IN THE FUTURE. CONSIDER THE FOLLOWING:
    A. INCREASE EFFORT
    B. CHANGE OR RETAIN GOALS
    C. ACCEPT THE CURRENT LEVEL OF PERFORMANCE AND CONTINUE TYPICAL EFFORTS
    D. CHANGE OR MAINTAIN THE SITUATION
    E. COMBINATION OF ALL OF THE ABOVE

cause and whether or not there is reason to expect the cause to occur again in the future. Similarly, the third step, comparing a person's performance with the performances of other people, provides the information that is necessary to determine whether or not the cause of an outcome is internal or external to the individual. The baseball example, the golf example, and the irate customer all illustrated how comparisons with others helped to determine whether the causes were internal or external.

The fourth step is the attribution process in which the information from the prior three steps is integrated to determine the most likely cause of the performance. Both information about the typical performances of other people as well as the consistency of performances over time were included in the golf example and the student example. In the golf example, it was concluded that since other weekend golfers had similar results and since the results were inconsistent over time (some good, some bad), the cause of poor performance was most likely due to the internal and unstable cause of lack of practice. On the other hand, the poor performance of the student was attributed to the internal and stable cause of lack of ability on integrative tests since the student consistently performed poorly on integrative tests (stable).

The last step is the action plan and is based on the CR process described in the prior steps. These specific actions can take several forms depending on the attributed cause of the performance. In many cases the actions needed are fairly clear. In the golf example, the reason for the inconsistent performance was the internal and unstable cause of a lack of practice. The solution was disciplined practice and this was undoubtedly the appropriate action plan if one accepted the performance standard that was initially adopted. However, as you may recall, that solution was not adopted because of realistic constraints on the availability of practice time. Thus, in that case, the goal of shooting in the 70s was abandoned in lieu of a more realistic goal: exercise and enjoyment.

In the student example, the attribution for the poor test performance was the internal and stable inability to perform well on integrative tests. Since ability is stable and unchanging, the student realigned his priorities and chose an alternative career goal that was more suited to his abilities. In the irate customer example, the solution was more psychological. In that case the cause of the problem was determined to be the external and unstable event of having an unreasonable customer that the employee could do nothing about. Therefore, the action plan was to accept the causal explanation that "every so often you get a customer that you cannot please, so you need to stop internalizing and blaming yourself for a lack of ability because it is not your fault." Thus, this action plan represents a change in attitude, but it is a very specific and calculated change in CR so that neither self-esteem nor performance is eroded.

Another alternative not discussed explicitly is changing the environment when the cause of poor performance is attributed to an external and stable factor that cannot be controlled. Thus, for example, one may conclude that one cannot attain a promotion because of a particular supervisor or performance environment. In the case of such stable and external causes, a rational solution is to change the environment (i.e., companies or supervisors) if possible.

Finally, action plans can be a combination of all four of the alternatives suggested above. In the golf example, goals could be modified while still increasing practice and accepting less than spectacular results based on the knowledge that the practice is still not sufficient. The important thing is to understand why performance is at a specific level, develop an action plan, maintain realistic expectations, and facilitate optimal performance by self-talk that maintains reasonable expectations and self-esteem within the constraints that are recognized.

In summary, action plans can result in: a.) very specific behavior changes such as increased practice; b.) changes in goals; c.) environmental changes; d.) acceptance and maintenance of current performance levels; and e.) a combination of all of the above. Assessing CR is the key to this process because it provides the analytic foundation and road map for the action plan. Reframing CR can be done as an individual project. Leaders, managers, coaches, teachers, and others who manage the behavior of others can also facilitate this process by familiarizing their charges with the road map and offering constructive feedback when they see someone taking a wrong turn.

STRUCTURED EXPERIENCES FOR GROUPS AND ORGANIZATIONS

The attributional retraining strategy described above was targeted toward changing individual CR styles on a one-to-one basis. Similar strategies can be used on a group and organizational basis to educate members about techniques and procedures for overcoming CR biases. Part of our Executive Development Program at Florida State University is a one-day workshop on leadership on Dog Island (weather permitting), which is a small island off the Gulf Coast of Florida that can only be reached by boat. At the beginning of this program, the participants complete questionnaires to identify CR style. They are then introduced to a new task, throwing a cast net (i.e., a circular net used to catch baitfish), which is a challenging and unfamiliar task for almost everyone. The technique is demonstrated. The participants are asked about their attributions, feelings, and expectations regarding their likelihood of success at the task. They practice and receive coaching on how to throw the net. Then they make ten throws. Finally, they are asked to draw pictures of their best and worst results and to describe to the group the reasons (i.e., attributions) for their best and worst casts.

After the participants describe their attributions for their best and worst casts, we discuss the principles described in this book emphasizing that their self-talk facilitates or hinders performance. We then talk about how they can make their self-talk more constructive and how they can use these same principles in coaching and developing their associates.

Similar techniques can be used in the classroom. One particularly effective strategy is to ask students about their best and worst test grades as a way of introducing the notions of CR. Prior to this discussion the students complete questionnaires to identify both their individual and observer CR styles. Similar to the conclusion of the Dog Island program, the session ends with a discussion of the steps the students can take to become less biased in their CR and encourage others to adopt less biased approaches.

Many additional exercises and workshops can be conducted to encourage objective CR. The general model for these programs is described in Table 10-2. Any challenging task such as golf, computer games, cooperative team exercises, and rock climbing can be used to help illustrate how CR self-talk influences performance.

CONCLUDING COMMENTS

The above list of suggestions for moving toward unbiased CR is not exhaustive. An understanding of the theory presented throughout the book should provide you with a foundation to take advantage of additional opportunities to develop beneficial CR processes. Obviously, any knowledge or education that allows you to more objectively assess yourself or others contributes to your ability to reduce CR biases. Moreover, there are many specific activities and behaviors that can also contribute to more objective CR, particularly if you are aware of the dynamics of the CR process that are described in this book.

In concluding, it is worthwhile once again to emphasize that the objectives of CR change processes depend upon the individual and the specific situation. Some theorists have suggested that an optimistic bias is the healthiest perspective. Although there is data that demonstrates the debilitating effects of pessimistic biases, up to this point there does not appear to be any data or research that unequivocally supports the merits of an optimistic bias for all situations. The position taken in this book is that the direction you want to move in depends on where you are and where you want to go. Clearly, depressed individuals who display pessimistic biases will want to move toward more optimistic styles. However, evidence that suggests that some criminals may have overly optimistic biases also suggests that moving toward more optimistic styles is not the solution for everyone. We all have to find our own way. Hopefully, the information presented here will assist you in reducing destructive biases that may affect your own CR processes and enable you to help others adopt CR processes that lead to more beneficial outcomes.

TABLE 10.2. A General Model for CR Workshops

1. ADMINISTER CR STYLE QUESTIONNAIRES TO ASSESS INDIVIDUAL AND OBSERVER CR STYLES
2. INTRODUCE A CHALLENGING TASK
3. HAVE THE PARTICIPANTS DESCRIBE THEIR EXPECTATIONS FOR SUCCESS, THEIR FEELINGS ABOUT THEIR LIKELY PERFORMANCE IN THE TASK, AND ATTRIBUTIONS FOR THEIR EXPECTED PERFORMANCE
4. PROVIDE INSTRUCTION AND AN OPPORTUNITY FOR PRACTICE
5. PERFORM THE TASK AND MEASURE RESULTS
6. ASSESS ATTRIBUTIONS FOR THEIR PERFORMANCES
7. DISCUSS CR PROCESSES, CR STYLES, AND THEIR IMPLICATIONS FOR BOTH CURRENT AND FUTURE PERFORMANCE
8. DEVELOP ACTION PLANS REGARDING CR PROCESSES THAT WILL FACILITATE FUTURE PERFORMANCE

KEY POINTS

1. Clarifying objectives, roles, evaluation procedures, and performance standards is one way of minimizing ambiguity and reducing bias.

2. Increasing physical and psychological closeness reduces biases.

3. Money usually has high hedonic relevance. To avoid the negative effects of hedonic relevance, create procedures to formalize events (e.g., mortgages, contracts, and ceremonies) so that they can be as objective and unbiased as possible.

4. Impression management strategies such as accounts, apologies, and information manipulation can help manage and reduce observer biases.

5. Attribution retraining is aimed at empowering oneself and empowering other people by replacing biased CR with emotionally intelligent CR that fosters self-esteem and facilitates reasonable expectations for success in the future.

6. Comparisons with other people are one of the primary sources of information that we use to determine whether or not success and failure are due to internal or external causes.

7. Comparing a current performance with past performances over time in the same types of situations provides the information that is needed to determine whether or not a cause is stable or unstable.

8. The exact words that you as a leader, coach, parent, or manager say to empower high performance depends on the person's CR in that specific situation and your knowledge of that situation.

CHAPTER XI

INTERPRETING THE SELF-TEST: PART II

Now that we have had a chance to see how CR biases affect the way we think about ourselves and others, the results of Part II of the self-test will be more meaningful.

Recent research has demonstrated that just as we have styles that affect how we view our own successes and failures (i.e., personal CR styles), we also have styles that reflect how we view the performances of others (i.e., social CR styles). In general, when we engage in CR about the performance of others, we use the same type of explanations (e.g., ability and effort) and the same types of dimensions (e.g., internal/external and stable/unstable) as we did when we engaged in attributions about our own performances. Just as CR about our own performance affects how we feel about our expectations, our behaviors, and ourselves, CR about the performance of others affects how we feel about them, our expectations regarding their future performance, and our behavior towards them. In general, when we believe that a person is performing poorly because of a lack of effort, we are more likely to hold the person responsible for the poor performance, be angry, punish the individual, and try to get them to do a better job the next time. On the other hand, when we believe that the cause of poor performance is due to a person's lack of ability, we are less likely to hold the person responsible, more likely to pity the person, less likely to try to punish the person, and less likely to encourage the person to try to do better the next time. When we attribute a person's poor performance to external factors such as a difficult task or bad luck, we are also less likely to blame and punish the person. Thus, social attributions about performance have important implications for how we feel and behave towards others.

Part II of the self-test was designed to provide a preliminary assessment of your social CR style. The same types of caveats that applied to considering the results of Part I of the self-test also apply to Part II. Again, the results are only an indication of your potential social CR style. Although similar questions on prior social CR style tests appear to be valid and reliable indications of social CR styles, the brevity of this test and the conditions under which it was taken (i.e., a self-test) make it difficult to be completely confident that it is reliable and valid. Nonetheless, the self-test is useful in suggesting and thinking about what your social CR style may be. Second, although measures of social CR styles are useful in predicting how you will react to the successes and failures of others, the specific person you are dealing with and the particular circumstances of the occasion will still be the most important influence on how you think about and react to someone else's successes and failures. More specifically, social CR styles represent tendencies to think in a particular way and people do not always follow their tendencies. For example, even though you may have a tendency to blame employees when they don't achieve the results you expect, it is unlikely that you would blame an employee for a failure to meet a sales quota in the week following a disastrous hurricane. Thus, like individual CR styles, social CR styles only suggest tendencies and do not predict how you will react to the performance of a peer, friend, or employee in a specific situation. However, over the long haul, the consistent biases represented by social CR styles will have an impact.

The procedures for scoring the self-test and the interpretations of the scores are provided below.

LOC SCORES

Locus of Causality (LOC) scores indicate the degree to which you attribute the successes and failures of other people to internal characteristics such as their ability and effort as opposed to external causes such as a difficult job or luck. High internal scores indicate that you tend to assign the responsibility for outcomes to the person you are observing whereas high external scores indicate a tendency to attribute the outcomes of other people to outside factors. The scores on this dimension are also important because they are related to how you feel about other people. High internal scores suggest that you tend to assign personal blame for failures and personal credit for successes whereas high external scores suggest that you are less likely to assign blame or credit to individuals for both unsuccessful and successful outcomes.

As the scoring procedures below suggest, not all people are consistent in how they think about other people's successes and failures and may attribute success to internal factors while attributing failure to external causes. In the second questionnaire that you took there were two success and two failure events. Items 1 and 2 assessed how you responded to failure events. Items 3 and 4 assessed how you reacted to success.

You can determine your own score by following the directions below:

LOC SCORES FOR SUCCESS EVENTS

1. Calculate the LOC scores for positive events by adding up the scores for the following items:

   3a. ____ + 3b. ____ + 3c ____ + 3d. ____ + 3e. ____
   + 4a. ____ +4b. ____ + 4c. ____ + 4d. ____ + 4e. ____
   = TOTAL ____

CIRCLE

> INTERNAL FOR SUCCESS EVENTS (if your score is above 35)
>
> EXTERNAL FOR SUCCESS EVENTS (if your score is 35 or below)

This score should be between 10 and 70 and indicates the degree to which you give other people credit for success and is an indication of social optimism. In general, if your score is above 35, you are a high internal positive, meaning that you give people credit for their successes and their successes make you feel positively toward them. If your score is 35 or below, you are a high external positive and you have a tendency to attribute the successes of others to the situation, luck, chance, or yourself.

LOC SCORES FOR FAILURE EVENTS

Calculate the LOC scores for negative events by adding up the scores for the following items:

1a.____ + 1b.____ + 1c.____ + 1d.____ + 1e.____
+ 2a.____ +2b ____ +2c.____ + 2d.____ + 2e.____
= Total _____

CIRCLE

> EXTERNAL FOR FAILURE EVENTS (if your score is above 35)
>
> INTERNAL FOR FAILURE EVENTS (if your score is 35 or below)

This score should also be between 10 and 70 and indicates the degree to which you hold people responsible for their failures and is an indication of social pessimism. In general, if your score is below 35, you have a strong tendency to make internal attributions for negative events, meaning that you tend to hold people responsible for their failures. As a result, you tend to have negative feelings towards people who fail. On the other hand, if your score is above 35, you tend to attribute peoples' failures to external factors. Thus you tend to blame the failure of others on something or someone besides the people themselves and may even blame yourself for the failures of others. An asset of the tendency to accept external explanations for the failures of others is that people generally perceive you as supportive. The liability is that people may take advantage of your apparent generosity. On the other hand, the liability of the tendency to make internal attributions for the failures of others is that people may avoid you because they believe that you are very critical. The positive side of this tendency to hold other people responsible for their failures is that they see you as demanding and try to meet your expectations if they believe that they can.

STABILITY SCORES

Stability scores are important because they are an indication of whether or not you believe that the cause of an outcome for someone is permanent or temporary. If the cause of a failure is believed to be stable and permanent as in the case of low ability or an extremely difficult task, you do not expect that additional effort by the person will lead to a different outcome in the future. As a result, you will probably do little to try to encourage or motivate the person. On the other hand, if the cause of a negative event is believed to be unstable and temporary as in the case of insufficient effort, you expect that with additional effort, the person will be able to succeed. Therefore, you are likely to be more proactive with this type of person, providing feedback and encouraging continued effort. Stable attributions for success increase the expectancy of future success whereas unstable attributions for success decrease expectations that future efforts by the person will pay off. Thus the stability dimension affects your expectations that the person will be successful in the future whereas the LOC dimension described previously affects how you feel about the other person.

Please follow the directions below to calculate your stability scores for social attributions:

Interpreting the Self-Test: Part II

STABILITY SCORE FOR SUCCESS EVENTS

Calculate the stability score for positive events by adding up the scores for the following items:

3a. ____ - 3b. ____ - 3c. ____ + 3d. ____ + 3f. ____
+ 4a. ____ - 4b. ____ -4c. ____ + 4d. ____ + 4f. ____
= Total _____
Scores should range from -11 to +19.

CIRCLE

STABLE FOR SUCCESS EVENTS (if your score is above 4)

UNSTABLE FOR SUCCESS EVENTS (if your score is 4 or below)

This score, as indicated above, suggests the degree to which you believe that a person's successes are due to stable causes such as their ability or an easy task. In general, if your score is above 4, you believe that when people experience positive events, they are caused by stable factors such as their ability or a good situation. Because of your belief in the stability of these causes, you also expect that these individuals will be successful in similar situations in the future and will do little to try to change the person or the situation. If your score is below 4, you tend to believe that the causes of people's successes are due to unstable factors such as high effort or luck and you tend to lack confidence that people will be successful in the future. Nonetheless, you may reward what you perceive to be extraordinary effort or luck and hope for the best in the future.

Stable attributions for success suggest an optimistic interpersonal CR style while attributing success to unstable causes is more indicative of a pessimistic interpersonal CR style.

STABILITY SCORE FOR FAILURE EVENTS

Calculate the stability score for failure events by adding up the scores for the following items:

-1a.____ + 1b.____ + 1c.____ -1d.____ - 1f.____
- 2a.____ +2b.____ +2c.____ - 2d.____ - 2f.____
= Total _____

Scores should range from -38 to +22.

CIRCLE

    STABLE FOR NEGATIVE EVENTS (if your score is above -8)

    UNSTABLE FOR NEGATIVE EVENTS (if your score is -8 or below)

As discussed above, this score suggests the degree to which you tend to believe that, in general, people fail because of stable causes such as a lack of ability or difficult tasks. In general, if your score is above -8, you indicated that when people experience the types of negative events described by the questionnaire, they were caused by stable factors. Because of your tendency to believe that the causes of people's failures are stable and enduring, you also expect that, in general, people who fail will have difficulties achieving success in similar situations in the future. As a result, you may often ignore people when they fail or fire them because you believe that they do not have the ability to do the job. If your score is -8 or below, you tend to believe that the causes of people's failures are due to unstable factors such as low effort or bad luck and you tend to believe that they will eventually achieve success because things may be different in the future. Thus you have a tendency to continue to be supportive of people who have not been productive in the past because you think that their situations, circumstances, or effort may change in the future.

OVERALL ASSESSMENT

By combining the above results you can derive your potential social CR style, which will be a combination of the two dimensions of the LOC and stability measures for both the success and failure scenarios. Please underline each of the dimensions you circled for each of the four scores that you derived.

1. internal/external for success events
2. internal/external for failure events
3. stable/unstable for success events
4. stable/unstable for failure events

Now that we have had some experience determining your social CR type, a more complete narrative description of each of the types is described in the next chapter.

DEFINITIONS

1. *Social CR Styles*—tendencies in the way we think about the successes and failures of others.

KEY POINTS

1. Social CR styles affect how we feel about others, our expectations regarding their future performance, and our behavior towards them.
2. Despite CR styles, the specific person you are dealing with and the particular circumstances are the most important influence on how you think about and react to someone else's successes and failures.
3. Over the long haul, the consistent biases represented by social CR styles will have an impact.

CHAPTER XII

THE SIXTEEN SOCIAL CR STYLES

At the onset, it is important to emphasize that the area of social CR styles is much less well researched than the notion of personal CR styles. Nonetheless, although limited, the research that has been done in this area confirms that there are consistent trends in how people evaluate the successes and failures of others that correspond to the explanations and dimensions described in the previous chapter. Thus, it makes logical sense to conclude that there are patterns of CR styles for evaluating the outcomes of others that match the patterns we use in evaluating our own outcomes. The social CR styles presented reflect the result of the logical extension of the theory. However, it is important to note that systematic research has not yet been conducted to validate the existence of each and every one of the styles described. Thus, the descriptions of the social CR styles are based on the logic of the theory rather than research that demonstrates the characteristics of people with these styles. Although these descriptions are speculative, this speculation is probably the best way to begin thinking about how the different CR dimensions interact. Despite the tentative nature of these descriptions, they are useful to theorists in that empirical testing could be conducted to determine whether or not people who score a particular way actually behave the way the descriptions suggest. For our purposes, they are useful in that they can help us begin to think about the styles we have in evaluating others and how they may be affecting the way we think about and treat other people.

THE HORSE TRAINER

People with this style tend to believe that there are born winners and losers and that success is a function of pedigree. They view both the successes and failures of other people as a function of the internal and stable characteristic of ability. People with this style try to associate themselves with talented people and believe that the key to a successful business or relationship is selecting the right person. They like to associate with other "winners" and they tend to believe that some people deserve more in life than others because they are "better" people. At times, individuals who adhere to this philosophy are snobbish and prejudiced against other persons or groups that they believe are less gifted.

Because of their belief that performance is the result of stable and internal characteristics such as ability, they make little effort to motivate or manage others. If things aren't working out, they are more likely to try to replace a person rather than attempt a motivational or rehabilitative strategy. The positive side of this perspective is that people with this style waste very little time with unproductive people. The negative side is that people with this style tend to ignore situational factors that may be causing performance problems.

THE SPLIT PERSONALITY

People with this style have a tendency to make internal and stable attributions for the success of others and reinforce success emphasizing the skills and abilities of their associates. However, when their associates fail, leaders with this style attribute the failure to internal and unstable characteristics such as inadequate effort. The positive side of this style is

TABLE 12.1. The Sixteen Social CR Styles

	SUCCESS ATTRIBUTIONS	FAILURE ATTRIBUTIONS
1. THE HORSE TRAINER	INTERNAL/STABLE (E.G., ABILITY)	INTERNAL/STABLE (E.G., LACK OF ABILITY)
2. THE SPLIT PERSONALITY	INTERNAL/STABLE (E.G., ABILITY)	INTERNAL/UNSTABLE (E.G., LACK OF EFFORT)
3. THE EMPATHIZER	INTERNAL/STABLE (E.G., ABILITY)	EXTERNAL/STABLE (E.G., ENVIRONMENT AND OTHER PEOPLE)
4. THE OPTIMIST	INTERNAL/STABLE (E.G., ABILITY)	EXTERNAL/UNSTABLE (E.G., BAD LUCK)
5. THE DISCREDITOR I	INTERNAL/UNSTABLE (E.G., EFFORT)	INTERNAL/STABLE (E.G., LACK OF ABILITY)
6. THE SLAVE DRIVER	INTERNAL/UNSTABLE (E.G., EFFORT)	INTERNAL/UNSTABLE (E.G., LACK OF EFFORT)
7. MR. OR MS. ARROGANT	INTERNAL/UNSTABLE (E.G., EFFORT)	EXTERNAL/STABLE (E.G., ENVIRONMENT AND OTHER PEOPLE)
8. THE CHEERLEADER	INTERNAL/UNSTABLE (E.G., EFFORT)	EXTERNAL/UNSTABLE (E.G., BAD LUCK)

9. THE FAULTFINDER	EXTERNAL/STABLE (E.G., EASE OF TASK)	INTERNAL/STABLE (E.G., LACK OF ABILITY)
10. THE BLAMER	EXTERNAL/STABLE (E.G., EASE OF TASK)	INTERNAL/UNSTABLE (E.G., LACK OF EFFORT)
11. ENVIRONMENTALIST	EXTERNAL/STABLE (E.G., EASE OF TASK)	EXTERNAL/STABLE (E.G., ENVIRONMENT AND OTHER PEOPLE)
12. MR. OR MS. GRAVYTRAIN	EXTERNAL/STABLE (I.E., EASE OF TASK)	EXTERNAL/UNSTABLE (E.G., BAD LUCK)
13. THE PESSIMIST	EXTERNAL/UNSTABLE (E.G., GOOD LUCK)	INTERNAL/STABLE (E.G., LACK OF ABILITY)
14. MR. OR MS. ABUSIVE	EXTERNAL/UNSTABLE (E.G., GOOD LUCK)	INTERNAL/UNSTABLE (E.G., LACK OF EFFORT)
15. MR. OR MS. INCONSEQUENTIAL	EXTERNAL/UNSTABLE (E.G., GOOD LUCK)	EXTERNAL/STABLE (E.G., ENVIRONMENT AND OTHER PEOPLE)
16. THE DISCREDITOR II	EXTERNAL/UNSTABLE (E.G., GOOD LUCK)	EXTERNAL/UNSTABLE (E.G., BAD LUCK)

that these types of leaders get along well with their employees when things are going well and they build momentum by reinforcing self-esteem as long as the good performance continues. In addition, they believe that everyone is capable if they exert enough effort. On the other hand, when associates are not doing well, they tend to blame the problems on the associates and may belittle the perceived lack of effort. Thus, rather than building self-esteem and problem solving, this type of leader may alienate associates by jumping to the conclusion that poor performance is due to a lack of effort.

THE EMPATHIZER

Leaders with this style give credit for successes to their associates by attributing the success to internal and stable characteristics such as ability. On the other hand, they tend to attribute the failures of their associates to stable and external causes such as an overly challenging and unfair task. Associates usually like these type of leaders because they build associates' self-esteem when things are going well by crediting the success to the associates' abilities. When things are going poorly, this type of leader protects associates' self-esteem by blaming the problems on the environment. The downside of this type is that because this type of leader protects self-esteem during failures, the associates are not encouraged to make accurate assessments of their problems and may never take responsibility for the problems they create. In addition, this type of leader may also be seen as taking the side of the employees and blaming the organization when things go wrong.

THE OPTIMIST

Leaders who have an optimistic view of their associates give them credit for success by making internal and stable attributions such as ability and blame associates' failures on external and unstable factors such as bad luck and chance. The positive side of this style is that the associates are almost never discouraged and their self-esteem is enhanced. The negative side is that the associates of optimists may fail to recognize their role in poor performance and, over the long haul, will fail to assume personal responsibility when it is warranted.

THE DISCREDITOR I

These types of discreditors attribute their associates' successes to unstable internal factors such as extraordinary effort, suggesting that their performances cannot be sustained over the long run. On the other hand, they tend to attribute associates' failures to internal and stable factors such as ability. These types of individuals are not uncommon in teaching and begrudgingly give A's to hard-working students but often communicate to the students that their performance still leaves something to be desired. Associates with these types of leaders feel that they are always "on trial" and have a hard time developing confidence because the leader rarely communicates positive expectations for future performance.

THE SLAVE DRIVER

Leaders with this style tend to believe that internal and unstable attributes such as effort are the cause of both successes and failures. Most importantly, they tend to believe that everyone has about the same ability and that exceptional performance is simply the result of exceptional effort. They believe that everyone can become president if they try hard enough. Because they tend to believe that extraordinary effort is necessary for success and any lapse in effort will result in failure, they may have a built-in fear of failure and constantly push and prod their associates for more effort. They tend to have the same philosophy about their own success, adopt a workaholic lifestyle, and expect their associates to do the same. They rarely stop to smell the roses and discipline anyone else who tries.

MR. OR MS. ARROGANT

Leaders with this style tend to attribute their employees' successes to internal and unstable causes such as effort and their failures to external and stable causes such as the environment or other people. These types of leaders leave their people feeling that their exceptional performances are never quite adequate and that they can make little difference when things go wrong. As a result, these leaders are often perceived as arrogant and aloof and their associates do not feel motivated to solve organizational problems. Consequently, they may not make the changes they need to make to fully develop their abilities and skills.

THE CHEERLEADER

People with this style tend to make internal and unstable attributions for their associates' successes such as extraordinary effort. Because these leaders are insecure and believe that organizational success is the result of extraordinary effort, they reward exceptional efforts and champion contests and other competitive activities to stimulate greater effort. Thus, even though their associates may be successful, they may not be confident that they will achieve success in the future because of feedback that tells them that the reasons for their successes are unstable. On the other hand, leaders with this style tend to attribute their associates' failures to external and unstable factors such as bad luck. Thus they may ignore staffing problems related to ability and believe that, as long as effort continues, luck will change and the organization will eventually become successful again. The downside of this type of leader is that they sometimes offend individuals by failing to recognize exceptional ability. Because they communicate to their people that both their successes and failures are caused by factors that are unstable, their people may have a tendency to be anxious because they do not believe that they can control their destinies. On the positive side, people with this style tend to have a very hands-on leadership style and usually can keep people interested and involved when things are going well.

THE FAULTFINDER

Leaders with this style tend to explain their associates' success with external and stable attributions such as an easy task. Thus they are unlikely to assign personal responsibility to their associates for success and rob them of the feelings of achievement that often accompany success. On the other hand, they tend to view their associates' failures as due to internal and stable causes such as a lack of ability. Because these types of leaders rarely give others any credit for success, and blames others for failures, it is hard to find a positive side for this type. In general, people do not like to work for faultfinders.

THE BLAMER

Like the faultfinder, the blamers tend to attribute their associates' successes to external and stable causes such as an easy task whereas they tend to attribute failures to internal and unstable factors such as a lack of effort. Blamers try to make their associates feel guilty when they do not perform well. In the short term they can generate acceptable performance by bullying people. Two things can happen to the associates of the blamer. If the associates have high self-esteem, they will eventually attribute their problems to a stable external cause (i.e., the blamer) and learn helplessness with respect to pleasing this type of boss. When this happens, employees shuffle through their day, say, "yes sir" and "no sir", and expend only enough efforts to keep out of trouble until they can find a better job. If they have low self-esteem, they will begin to believe the boss and become helpless and hapless go-fers.

THE ENVIRONMENTALIST

Leaders with this style believe that both success and failure are due to stable characteristics of their environment. They tend not to assign either credit or blame to their associates. Because they believe the environment is so important, they spend little time trying to develop their people and tend to be externally oriented and aloof from their associates. The upside is that associates are not blamed when things go wrong. On the other hand, they do not receive much credit for the successes of the organization.

MR. OR MS. GRAVYTRAIN

Leaders with this style believe that their associates' successes are due to external and stable characteristics such as a supportive organization and environment. Therefore, they do not attribute any responsibility to their associates and feel that they are all fortunate to have such a good job. On the other hand, when associates fail, these types of leaders tend to attribute the failure to external and unstable causes such as bad luck. As a result, they do not blame their associates or dwell on the failures since they believe that luck will change. These types of bosses are generally easy to get along with but they fail to build confidence or self-esteem in their employees and do not encourage them to develop their full potential.

THE PESSIMIST

Leaders with this style tend to attribute the successes of their associates to external and unstable causes such as chance and luck. As a result, they fail to give their associates credit for their successes and, since luck changes, they tend to expect the worst in the future. Moreover, because their associates' successes are believed to be the result of temporary and uncontrollable causes such as luck, they do little to try to motivate or develop their employees. With respect to failure, they believe that their associates' failures are due to lack of ability. It would be typical of these types of bosses to say that their employees are stupid and worthless. As a result, their condescending attitude and behaviors lead to poor interpersonal relations. Because they believe that their employees and associates lack ability, they make no effort to try to educate or train their employees. Thus, these types of leaders believe that there is little they can do to replicate their associates' successes in the future and may feel helplessness with respect to having an impact on their associates. Moreover, as discussed in Chapter Five, the feedback that these types of leaders give to their associates (that they have no ability and are not responsible for organizational successes) can also lead to learned helplessness in their employees. Thus pessimistic leaders are the architects of self-fulfilling prophecies.

MR. OR MS. ABUSIVE

Leaders who display this style attribute their employees' successes to external and unstable characteristics such as luck. They attribute associates' failures to internal and unstable causes such as poor effort or unreliability. These types of leaders erode the self-esteem of their employees because they fail to give them any credit for success. On the other hand, they hold the employees totally responsible for failure, blaming failures on causes such as laziness and lack of effort. They do almost nothing to encourage their employees to perform because they believe that their employees have little control over the factors that lead to high performance. However, they blame and abuse their people when things go wrong. Like the employees of the pessimist, employees managed by Mr. or Ms. Abusive may become depressed and helpless with respect to their ability to please their bosses. Hopefully, they do not generalize their feelings to their jobs and to the whole company.

MR. OR MS. INCONSEQUENTIAL

People with this style tend to attribute employee successes to external and unstable causes such as luck. Because these leaders do not feel that their employees have earned their successes, they tend to denigrate their associates and fail to give them credit for achievements. On the other hand they do not blame their employees for failure because they attribute it to the external and stable characteristics of the environment or other people. Thus, people with these types of bosses never feel that they are a part of a team. They may be in awe of the boss or the company if the company is successful, but, if they buy into their boss's feedback, they do not feel that they are part of the action. On the other hand, when they recognize this type of pattern in their boss, they are likely to see their boss as a selfish person who cannot be pleased and who fails to share the fruits of success.

THE DISCREDITOR II

This type of discreditor attributes associates' successes to external and unstable sources such as good luck, failing to give them credit for their efforts or abilities. When they fail, this type of boss also blames external and unstable sources such as bad luck, failing to hold employees responsible and accountable, even when it is their fault. As a result, employees with this type of boss learn helplessness with respect to receiving credit for their work. Eventually, they may begin to believe that they have little control or responsibility for the organization's successes or failures. Their only motivation to work will be to receive their paycheck.

Once again it is important to emphasize that these descriptions are based on theory rather than actual studies of people whose assessment placed them in these categories. Moreover, because the theory regarding the effects of attribution styles on interpersonal interactions is not well developed, these types of descriptions are even more tentative than those that were given for the effects of attributions styles on self-motivation. Nonetheless, these descriptions are offered to help us think about how our styles affect other people. Hopefully, comparing your style to the stereotypical descriptions provided here will help you maximize your potential to motivate others and minimize the negative effects that your style could have on others.

CHAPTER XIII

MANAGING INTERPERSONAL CR STYLES

In this chapter we will consider options for managing interpersonal CR styles. First, we will review and apply what we have already learned about managing our own intrapersonal biases to managing interpersonal biases. Then, we will look specifically at interventions designed to manage personal and organizationally-induced helplessness.

In Chapter Nine we discussed procedures for overcoming biased CR self-attribution styles. Since the biases in self-appraisal are part and parcel of the interpersonal styles we described, many of the methods for overcoming the negative effects of interpersonal styles are essentially the same. The techniques discussed in Chapter Nine included: removing ambiguity, reframing to control the effects of hedonic relevance, developing empathy, increasing interaction and physical proximity, and using impression management, multiple raters, and attributional counseling.

The difference in applying the suggestions offered in Chapter Nine to interpersonal styles is a matter of perspective. In Chapter Nine the objective was to control the biases you had with respect to your own performance. The objective is still very similar, but now you have two objectives. The first is to manage the biases you have about other people's performances. The second is to manage the environment so that the associates or colleagues that you are observing can also make objective assessments of their own performance. The basic notion is that if you can optimize the objectivity that both you and the performers have in assessing their performance, you will be able to minimize the negative affects of biased interpersonal styles.

With respect to managing ambiguity, now your goal is to establish objective performance standards so that both you and your associates can agree on the characteristics of high, moderate, and low performance. One of the best ways of doing this is to establish the performance standards participatively. The advantage of this type of process is that the members of the group would help identify both positive and negative factors that would affect their abilities to accomplish their goals. Open discussion of these influences on performance would help ensure that the manager considers these factors when evaluating performance but also that the employees would keep these factors in mind before taking credit for successes or denying blame for failure. As an example of this strategy, consider a regional manager for a pharmaceutical sales company. The regional manager could dictate goals for each of the territory representatives. If the sales manager does this, because she has not had the benefit of either feedback or discussion, it is possible that the goals are too ambitious or too low because she would not have the same detailed knowledge that her people have regarding the differences, advantages, and disadvantages of each of the sales territories. As a result, there would be some disagreement and ambiguity as to whether or not one versus another territory representative had done a commendable job. On the other hand, if all of the factors that influence sales in the various territories are discussed openly and goals are set based on the characteristics of the various products and the sales territories, it is more likely that the manager and the representative will agree on their assessments of performance. Similarly, it is more likely that an open discussion like the one suggested would result in different goals for each of the territories that reflect their unique characteristics. Most importantly, when something goes wrong, as will inevitably happen at some point, both the manager and the sales representative have already discussed the factors that could influence the performance. As a result, they have a solid ground for objective analyses.

Similar group processes would also be helpful in complementing the other suggestions for managing bias. More specifically, with respect to hedonic relevance, open group discussions would help to clarify the personal stake and investment that both managers and employees have in achieving or not achieving goals, making it less likely that biases would come into play. Similarly, open discussions and consensus on goals would stimulate more physical and psychological proximity, empathy, and the impression that management is considering all relevant factors (which would be an accurate impression). This procedure would result in feedback from multiple sources that would satisfy the criteria of multiple raters. Finally, open discussions of performance criteria, and of organizational and personal strengths and weaknesses, would help provide the type of in-depth analysis needed for attributional counseling.

In addition to applying the strategies discussed in Chapter Nine, there are also other ways of dealing with biases in others. They include ignoring the biases, diagnosing the problem and providing objective feedback, leveling, and using an objective third party.

IGNORING THE BIAS

I once worked with a colleague (we'll call him Tom) who seemed totally oblivious to the politics of his environment. I vividly recall a meeting Tom and I attended during which a supposed group of allies was attempting to cut us out of the picture for a large consulting job. After the meeting, Tom and I had lunch and when he did not address the issues raised in the meeting, I asked him if he saw what the other group was attempting to do. Tom claimed total ignorance and after discussing the meeting with him, it was obvious that he was totally oblivious to the threat that the other group posed. Later, my gut feelings were realized, but we were able to avoid any negative impacts because I had already taken steps to ensure our viability in the project. Tom and I have remained good friends and because of this early incident, I have been more attuned to a consistent pattern in his behavior—he seems almost insensitive to other people's motives but is nonetheless able to singlemindedly pursue his own goals. As a result, Tom has been very successful and has been able to remain completely apolitical. I have never known Tom to be the source of anyone's personal attack and have never heard Tom attack anyone else.

Tom is a perfect illustration of the notion that ignoring other people's biases, innuendos, and even greed while maintaining your own goals is oftentimes the best strategy. Sometimes the problem does go away when you ignore it. As my mother used to say, "Some people are just looking for a fight. You don't have to be the one that gives it to them."

LEVELING

Leveling is the opposite of ignoring. In many cases people are unaware of their own biases. In other situations, people intentionally conceal their motives and biases. As a result, biases often appear as hidden agendas that underlie the surface meaning of a message. Thus, a manager may reprimand an employee for a mistake, but the underlying reason for the reprimand is the manager's self-serving bias, trying to blame his or her own failure on the employee.

In leveling, the party who is the object of the bias brings the bias to the surface, forcing the perpetrator to address the real purpose of the message. Thus, for example, an employee who is unnecessarily and repeatedly reprimanded may respond by asking "Are you trying to help me so that I don't make this mistake again or are you trying to say that I am totally responsible for this problem when it is clear that if management had given me the time and tools I needed, we wouldn't have this problem?" Obviously this is a risky strategy and is not recommended for all or even most cases. However, leveling is sometimes needed to stop destructive interpersonal games and to force others to confront their biases. A major problem, however, is that, if the boss is playing a game and refuses to stop even after being confronted, you may have to start looking for a new job. Similarly, confronting an employee with his or her biases may result in a grievance, retaliation of some kind, or a resignation. Thus, leveling is most often the last resort, but can be a very effective strategy for stopping destructive games.

DIAGNOSING THE BIAS AND PROVIDING HELPFUL FEEDBACK

Another less confrontational strategy is to diagnose the other person's biases and provide feedback that helps allay his or her insecurities. In many cases, because of people's positions as observers or actors, they may simply not be aware of all of the factors that are affecting performance. Thus, as suggested in the section on impression management from Chapter Nine, accounts are often effective because they make observers aware of factors that they may be inadvertently ignoring. In the case of a manager giving unreasonably critical feedback, the employee may accept the feedback but carefully point out how situational factors (which the manager could have anticipated) contributed to the problems. Similarly, in the case involving Tom mentioned above, more carefully outlining our intentions and ensuring the competing group that they would get their share of the pie might have allayed the aggressiveness of the opposing group.

OBJECTIVE THIRD PARTIES

Occasionally, because of their biases, it is impossible for two parties to reach consensus on a fair evaluation of a situation. Our society has developed remedies for these types of problems. They include judges, grievance procedures, negotiators, ombudsmen, and mediators. From the theoretical perspective of this book, the job of the third party is to be objective, to accurately consider the perspectives of both parties when their perceptions differ. While it is often the case that third parties do a great job, this does not always happen. At least part of the reason that this process may be inadequate is that the third party views the situation from an observer's perspective, with both of the grieving parties as actors. As a result, third parties may be biased toward attributing the causes of grievances to the dispositional characteristics of the grievants and less likely to identify situational and environmental causes. This analysis suggests that third parties may not always be objective because they may not always search as diligently as possible to find environmental solutions. On the other hand, it also suggests that those who find themselves in third-party positions should attempt to do a purposeful environmental analysis in an attempt to find solutions for conflicts. Finally, it implies that the best solution to differing perceptions between two parties lies in the abilities of the two parties to suspend their biases and evaluate the situation objectively, since they know more about the situation than anyone else.

MANAGING HELPLESSNESS

In Chapter Nine we discussed a variety of things that can be done to manage intrapersonal biases, but did not address specific ways of addressing helplessness behaviors. Now that we have been able to see how both intrapersonal and interpersonal biases affect behavior, we can begin to understand why individuals become passive and helpless and how we can reduce the likelihood of helpless behaviors.

As we described earlier, learned helplessness results when individuals attribute their failures to internal and stable characteristics such as their ability. When people make internal and stable attributions for failure, they often feel depressed and hopeless. They feel bad because they believe it is their fault (i.e., internal attribution). They feel hopeless because they see the problems as continuing (i.e., stable attribution).

An objective analysis of the reasons for failure, suggested by the discussion in Chapter Three and Figure 3.1, indicates that the reasons for failure fall into four major categories. People fail because of: 1.) stable and internal causes such as their own lack of ability; 2.) unstable and internal causes such as their lack of effort; 3.) stable and external causes such as an extremely difficult task; 4.) external and unstable causes such as luck and chance; or some combination of the four categories.

The key to understanding learned helplessness is that, regardless of the actual cause of failure, people who are learned helpless believe that their internal and stable attributes are the primary cause of their failures. Thus, a new employee may attribute his failure to a lack of ability and become depressed even though a more accurate analysis of the reason for the failure might be that the task was too difficult. Similarly, an investor may attribute failure in the stock market to a lack of ability when the failure in a specific stock is actually due to a change in market conditions that could not have been anticipated. Thus the key to overcoming learned helplessness is to help people move from internal and stable attributions for failure to any of the other possibilities.

There are at least six specific strategies that can reduce the likelihood of learned helplessness in individuals.

Immunization

Immunization involves pre-treating individuals with success experiences so that they begin a pattern of attributions that facilitate productive behavior. Thus, for example, a sales manager may prequalify leads for new salespeople so that they experience success and believe that their sales are a function of their abilities. Similarly, many athletic teams schedule easy opponents at the beginning of the season to reinforce the teams' beliefs in their abilities. Thus, immunization is any pre-treatment with success to begin the process of productive and functional attributions before pessimistic attributions have the opportunity to become ingrained. After experiencing success, people are much more able to deal with failure.

Discrimination Training

Individuals often learn helplessness because of their experiences with no-win situations. Then, when situations change, they fail to recognize that the situation has changed and still act the same way. Many Americans found that the quality and efficiency of many U.S. cars was inferior to many of the imports during the late 1970's and were punished by poor quality and inefficiency. Since then, there have been many improvements in efficiency and quality by U.S. manufacturers, but many customers have learned helplessness because of their past experiences. They still have the same biases against domestic cars. They do not perceive that the situation has changed. In discrimination training, you try to help people discriminate between the old and the new situation. Thus the "this is not your father's Oldsmobile" commercial campaign several years ago appears to be predicated on prior helplessness by emphasizing the difference between the old conditions and the new situation. Similarly, organizations can alleviate helpless attributions by emphasizing that the situations and conditions have changed. Banks can emphasize that credit requirements have changed and that the likelihood of loans has increased substantially. Leaders can emphasize that they have changed and really want employee feedback.

Perceptions of Rewards

Part of the experience of learned helplessness is the belief that rewards are unavailable because they are not controllable. Another strategy is to change expectations of rewards from a situation of uncontrollability to one of controllability. More specifically, by demonstrating that rewards are tied to effort and performance, conditions of helplessness can be alleviated. Thus, policies, manuals, and communications that describe rewards for specific behaviors can be very helpful. An example would be the publication and dissemination of a tuition reimbursement program that describes the procedures for reimbursement as well as the likelihood of promotion when an employee completes a college education.

Modeling

Another strategy closely linked to discrimination training and perceptions of rewards is the use of models to demonstrate the changed conditions and opportunities for rewards. Publicizing people who have succeeded in achieving organizational goals such as completing a college education through a tuition reimbursement program is an example. In general, it has been found that models are most successful when people can identify with the model so that they believe that their experiences could be similar.

Ego Defense

One explanation for the debilitating effects of learned helplessness is that it is caused by the loss of self-esteem. When people believe that the causes of their failures are due to their own lack of ability, their self-esteem is eroded and they lose hope. Therefore, feedback should be carefully worded and specific to a particular performance. For example, giving a salesperson feedback about the specific things she needed to do (i.e., behaviors) in attempting to make a specific sale is far different that general feedback telling her that she is "incapable of closing a sale." Thus, to the extent that feedback about poor performance is related to specific behaviors, it should be far less damaging to self-esteem than feedback referring to general abilities.

Attribution Counseling

Attribution counseling can be considered any feedback designed to help a person overcome the types of pessimistic attributions that lead to learned helplessness and develop more realistic perceptions of causation. Thus, the goal of attribution counseling is usually to move a person's overall attribution process from pessimistic to more optimistic attributions. This can be done through professional counselors but it can also be done by correcting individuals when they make inappropriate internal and stable attributions for failures. An example is a teacher interacting with a student who has failed a test. From a counseling perspective, the teacher should work with the student to identify all of the possible causes for the poor performance. These causes could include not coming to class, failing to take proper notes, not reading the book, not studying hard enough, not studying the right things, misunderstanding the course content, and a lack of intellectual capacity. In most cases, the reasons for failure are not due to intellectual capacity but are due to one or several of the other factors. Helping the student to identify all of the possible problem areas and devise a plan for the next test is an example of attributional counseling. Similarly, leaders in work settings can and should help to identify the causes of failures and encourage employees to address those that are controllable.

ORGANIZATIONALLY- INDUCED HELPLESSNESS

It is also important to understand that there are oftentimes good reasons for people's perceptions of helplessness. Organizations and the external environment often impose no-win situations on their members. Examples of external environmental conditions that affect the probability of success in work organizations include economic conditions, social climate, technological changes, and political situations. Within organizations, the probabilities of success for the members are influenced by the organizations' structures, rules, procedures, appraisal systems, the nature of supervision, and the nature of the jobs themselves. Thus organizations may be seen as a major causal factor in learned helplessness.

As a result of the forces listed above, many employees often react, but they are not necessarily learned helpless. For example, one of the explanations for the violence in the U.S. Post Office system is the inflexible rules and work procedures. Employees who are learned helpless attribute the cause of their negative outcomes (e.g., failures to receive promotions and raises) to internal and stable characteristics such as their own ability. As a result they are likely to become depressed and exhibit poor work performance. On the other hand, employees in some cases will attribute the causes of their negative outcomes to the external and stable characteristics of the organization such as inflexible supervisors and unreasonable rules. These employees will feel trapped and the resulting frustration may then lead to anger and violence. Thus, aggression and violence may be seen as a result of stable and external attributions that lead to feelings of uncontrollability. Violence may be seen as an attempt by the employee to seize control and/or leave the situation.

Other possible attributions for negative work outcomes are unstable attributions that are either internal (e.g., lack of ability) or external (e.g., luck and chance). While luck and chance are not controllable, at least the individuals with this type of attribution do not feel that failures in the future are inevitable. Similarly effort can be changed and redirected. As a result, people who make effort attributions for failures usually attempt to change their own behavior rather that striking out against the organization.

Based on the above discussion, there are several things that managements can do to alleviate reactions to "no-win" environments. First and foremost, to the extent possible, they need to remove the barriers and change the conditions that create the perceptions and attributions that failure is inevitable. Thus, an audit of policies, compensation and promotional procedures, and supervisory styles is an important first step. Second, in the case where factors are beyond the control of the organization, education and participation can be helpful. Thus, stock purchasing programs encourage employees to pay attention to all of the factors that affect a company's profitability. Similarly, participation on company-wide committees such as grievance and quality control committees encourage members to consider the "big picture." Third, and most importantly, they must help members see a way out of negative conditions. More specifically, violence and aggression appear to be caused by stable external attributions. Although managers may not be able to change conditions affecting employees' situations, they can help by pointing out options. For example, an employee with a physically punishing job may be encouraged to try for a transfer. In extreme cases, a sympathetic boss may agree that conditions will not change and help an employee find a better job elsewhere. Most importantly, managers want to help employees perceive that failure is not inevitable (i.e., stable). Thus, in the case of learned helpless individuals, managers want to coach employees to consider the things that could change so that success could be possible. Likewise, helping employees see more possibilities may help the potentially aggressive employees who blame external and stable aspects of their environments for their failures.

In closing this chapter, it is important to recall the earlier theme of a realistic attribution style. As we said, the very best leaders are able to accurately size up their environment, communicate their vision to their people, and initiate the actions necessary to take advantage of the opportunities. In many ways, all of the strategies suggested for counseling people who may be learned helpless or aggressive have to do with changing their perspectives and perceptions from seeing a stable and static world that predestines failure, to seeing a more open system where change is possible. Making people more aware of their options so that they feel less trapped plays a major role in this process. In many ways, these summary comments reflect Seligman's suggestion that a slightly optimistic attribution style is most beneficial. If you are optimistic, you do not see the failures in your world as stable and static but as malleable and changing. Communicating that view is a major part of what leaders do for people.

DEFINITIONS

1. *Leveling*—when the party who is the object of the bias brings the bias to the surface, forcing the perpetrator to address the real purpose of a message.

2. *Immunization*—pre-treating individuals with success experiences.

3. *Discrimination Training*—interventions designed to help people discriminate between an old and a new situation.

4. *Attribution Counseling*—any feedback designed to help a person overcome dysfunctional attributions and develop more realistic perceptions of causation.

5. *Organizationally-Induced Helplessness*—The notion that organizational factors (e.g., structures, rules, procedures, appraisal systems, and the nature of supervision) and the external environment (e.g., economic conditions, social

climate, technological changes, and political situations) can sometimes impose failure on an organization's members.

KEY POINTS

1. You can minimize the negative affects of biased interpersonal styles by establishing objective performance standards.

2. The best solution to differing perceptions between two parties lies in the abilities of the two parties to suspend their biases and evaluate the situation objectively, since they know more about the situation than anyone else.

3. The key to overcoming learned helplessness is to help people move from internal and stable attributions for failure to any of the other possibilities.

4. Models are most successful when people can relate to the model.

5. Specific feedback about poor performance is far less damaging to self-esteem than general feedback.

6. The very best leaders are able to accurately size up their environment, communicate their vision to their people, and initiate the actions necessary to take advantage of the opportunities.

CHAPTER XIV

THE BIG PICTURE

A major goal of this book was to go beyond the prototype airport paperbacks that give 10 overly simplistic steps for personal and managerial success. At this point, we should have an in-depth understanding of our own CR styles, the styles of others who we interact with, and understand how these styles impact our ability to produce high performance in our daily social and work lives. While a major tenet of this book is that understanding your style and others' styles is at the heart of your ability to achieve at your highest levels, it is obvious that there are many other factors that affect achieving and facilitating optimal performance. The objective of this chapter is to place what we have learned about CR into the more general context of motivated behavior.

TOWARD A MODEL OF OPTIMAL PERFORMANCE

A general model of human motivation is illustrated in Figure 14.1. The model is a paradigm, based on decades of research on human motivation. Most psychologists would support the major components of the model, although there might be some argument about the labeling. Essentially, the model indicates that achievement-oriented behavior is the result of the interaction between the individual and the environment. The individual assesses the current situation (i.e., CR), recalls past successes and failures, develops an expectation of the likely outcomes for the particular situation, determines how to behave (i.e., sets a goal), behaves, and is either rewarded or punished as a result of the consequences of the behavior.

Some comment on the specific portions of this model help put our theory of CR into perspective.

The Environment

The environment offers opportunities for success. Although there can be little doubt that Coach Bowden is one of the finest college football coaches in the nation, if not the finest, he could not do what he does without a supportive environment. Nevertheless, the environment does not explain his success entirely. In my interview with Coach Bowden, he stressed the importance of a supportive environment and emphasized the things he did to negotiate and create an environment where he could succeed. More specifically, he came to Florida State because he was able to recognize an environment that would provide him with the opportunity he needed to succeed. Second, he worked with the boosters and the administration to create the resources he needed for the program. Finally, he has devoted a large proportion of his time in the off-season to recruiting, so that he has the players (i.e., the environment) that he needs to succeed.

Like Coach Bowden, other high performers are able to recognize the opportunities their environments offer, change their environments to make them more favorable, and constantly work in maintaining their environments to continue to provide opportunities. A major tenet of this book is that CR is at the heart of high performers' abilities to assess themselves, their environments, and the types of consequences they can generate with their behavior. An unbiased CR style is a prerequisite for identifying achievable goals and making the adjustments necessary to stay on track.

The Individual

We all have our strengths and weaknesses. Some people are smarter, some are more athletic, and some are better looking than others. Others are good at math but do poorly at

SITUATION **PERSON** **CONSEQUENCES**

Environment
- Physical Characteristics
- Other People

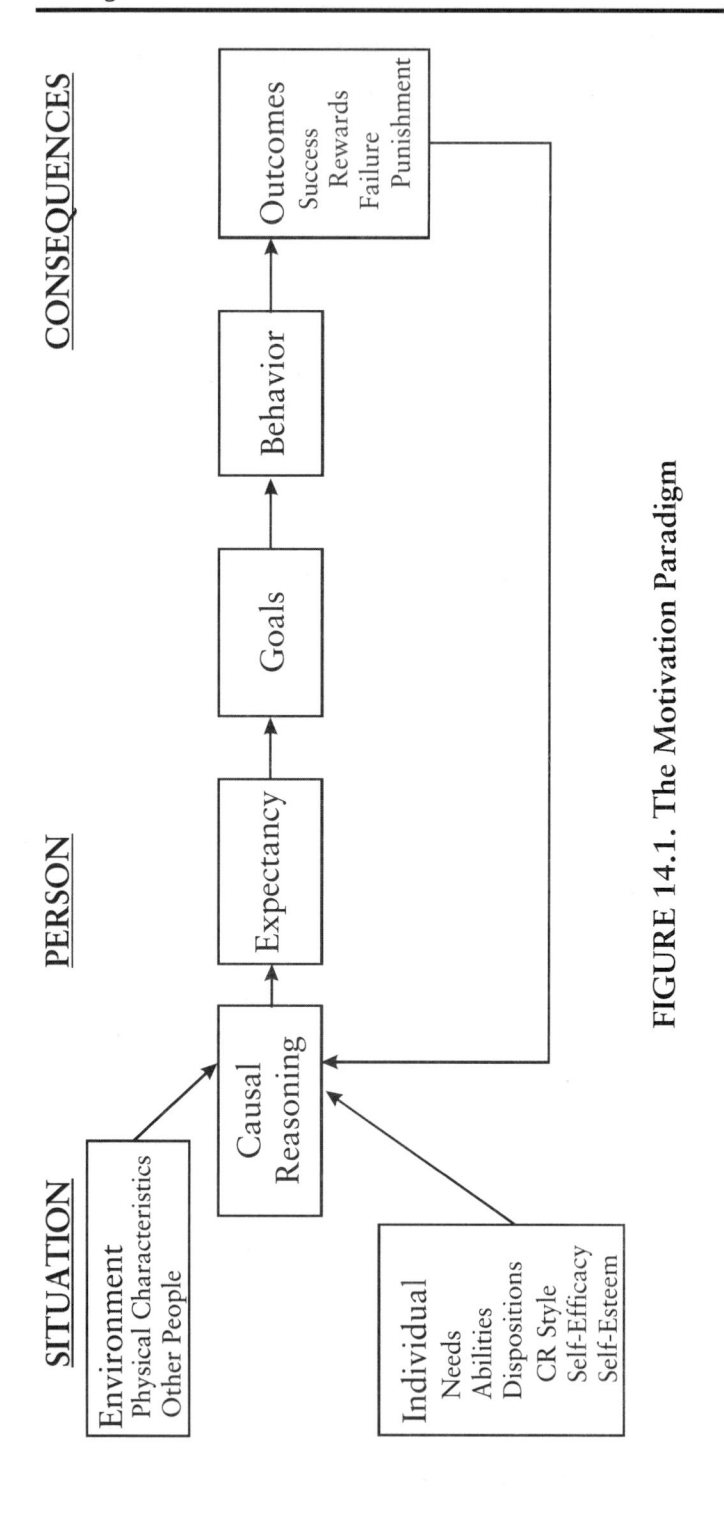

Individual
- Needs
- Abilities
- Dispositions
- CR Style
- Self-Efficacy
- Self-Esteem

Causal Reasoning → Expectancy → Goals → Behavior → Outcomes
- Success
- Rewards
- Failure
- Punishment

FIGURE 14.1. The Motivation Paradigm

reading. Some people excel in school but do poorly at practical tasks. Some managers excel in seeing the big picture but are poor at following through with the details. Obviously, these differences are important in determining who succeeds and who fails and must be recognized in our model of motivation. Clearly, with all things equal, a person with more talent and ability will outperform the one who does not have the talent. However, raw talent does not always dictate the level of performance. The question we have been asking throughout the book is "Given two people with equal talents and abilities, why does one perform better than the other?" From our perspective, the key is an objective CR style that enables you to recognize your strengths and weaknesses and find environments and opportunities where you can be successful. One of the more insightful concepts to emerge in the area of leadership is the notion of "substitutes for leadership." The basic notion is that there are many things that can take the place of direct leader behavior. Policies, procedures, rules, and regulations take the place of direct leader behaviors. Similarly, a leader who is weak in interpersonal skills can hire an assistant manager or public relations person to handle sensitive interpersonal matters and communications. Thus, if you have an objective assessment of your weaknesses, they can be overcome by making sure that you have the environment and the support you need.

Again, from our perspective, individuals who perform at optimal levels are able to objectively analyze themselves and their environments and set realistic goals so that they are able to generate the behaviors that they need to be successful. While there are many individual variables that affect success, CR style, self-esteem, and self-efficacy are listed specifically because they relate to self-awareness and the ability to construct an objective image of the self and how the self fits into the environment.

CAUSAL REASONING

Since the entire book is about CR, only some short commentary is necessary in this section.

As we have discussed, it appears that a key characteristic differentiating optimal versus average and poor performers is their ability to analyze themselves and their environments. If we view success and performance as a game, it becomes clear that the more knowledgeable participants are the most successful. However, life is not a game. There is no single goal or pay-off that everyone is attempting to achieve. Everyone can win and they do so by understanding what they need to do to realize their potential and optimize the payoffs that they value. Understanding your environment, your strengths and weaknesses, the payoffs that are available, and the probabilities of achieving your goals are undeniable prerequisites for consistent success.

At this point, you may be experiencing some hesitation in relating to the model and what may seem like a fairly mechanical and academic explanation of human motivation. You may be tempted to say that people are not so systematic and analytic and you are correct. Most people are not so systematic and analytic—just the optimal performers. Here are some examples:

1. Professional tennis players are so focused and analytical that they can actually see and explain the spin on the ball. They see the strokes of their opponents and know exactly how to stroke the ball on their return to overcome the spin from their opponent.

2. Professional basketball and football players spend hours analyzing film to identify their own and their opponent's strengths and weaknesses. They also spend hours in practice perfecting moves for particular situations and develop specific strategies to overcome their weaknesses.

3. Interviews with professional golfers demonstrate the remarkable analytic recall of these athletes. The golfers can almost always recall the hole, course conditions, and other details during post tournament interviews. Most everyday hackers can hardly remember their score on their home course let alone

recall the details of the grain in the green on a specific hole.

4. Successful investors such as Warren Buffet almost always have a detailed strategy for accomplishing their investment goals. Understanding the market and the strengths and weaknesses of their analytic procedures allows these investors to succeed while others are failing.

5. World class chess players can recall 24 of the 26 positions on the board if momentarily shown a midgame set-up on a board, even though it is not a game they are playing.

6. Accomplished builders can look at a blueprint and immediately visualize the completed structure whereas the average person may not know how the final project will look until it is complete, despite looking at the prints for months.

7. Professional bowlers differentiate lanes by how they are oiled and almost always know if there is an imperfection in the lane. The average bowler simply does not observe these differences.

8. White–water kayakers read the water and know what dangers lie beneath. The average person has no clue.

The reason these optimal performers recognize these small nuances is that they are all part of the complex of variables that must be attended to in order to generate optimal performance. They know that the variables that affect their performance can be internal or external and may be either stable or unstable. Most importantly, however, they attend to these cues and analyze them objectively.

Expectancies

Expectancies are the probabilities that one can produce the behaviors required for success as well as the probability that the behaviors will result in the desired rewards. When we expect that we can be successful, we are more likely to be motivated to engage in motivated behaviors and set goals that are challenging.

Again, we may be tempted to say that most people are not that analytic. Once again, it is true that most people are not that analytic—except for the optimal performers. I recall watching a basketball game with a professional gambler. There were about five minutes left in the game and he told me what the final score would be, explaining how a series of intentional fouls and foul shots would determine the score. And he was exactly right. It was clear to me that I was merely a spectator and that he was truly a professional. He saw much more than I did and he was able to estimate the most likely outcome.

In a similar manner, accomplished businesspeople, investors, contractors, lawyers, and athletes are all able to estimate the likelihood of their successes at the various projects they elect to undertake. Likewise, they know how much effort and resources they will need to muster to gain the intended rewards. Again, from our theoretical perspective, they are able to do this because of an unbiased CR style that allows them to understand the factors (i.e., internal/external; stable/unstable) that are likely to affect their chances of succeeding.

Goal Setting

Goal setting is probably the most highly researched motivational phenomena. Unlike many areas of the behavioral sciences, the results of this research are crystal clear: 1.) people who set goals outperform people who don't set goals; 2.) specific goals result in higher levels of performance than general goals; and 3.) challenging goals result in higher levels of performance than easy goals. Research on high need achievers demonstrates that, as opposed to others, they set realistic but challenging goals. Within the context of CR theory, optimal performers are able to set these types of goals because they have analyzed the causes of their performance including the environment (external) and their own strengths and weaknesses (internal). As a result, they are able to make reasonably accurate estimates of the probabilities of their successes. Again, an unbiased CR style appears to be a key component of this process.

It should also be noted that high-performing leaders perform the same goal setting functions for their work units. Following the same model, these managers are able to accurately assess the opportunities and challenges in their environments, match the opportunities with the strengths and weaknesses of their people, estimate probable successes, and set challenging but achievable goals thereby empowering their people to obtain optimal performance levels.

Behaviors

Behaviors are the foundation of our model and the things we are trying to motivate. We define behaviors as observable activities; not thoughts, perceptions, or possibilities. By defining behaviors this way, we keep our model grounded in observable reality. There are several aspects of this portion of our model that need emphasis.

First, because behaviors ground our model in reality, motivation is not entirely a perceptual state. We can see motivated behavior by measuring its frequency and quality. Moreover, because of the physical properties of motivated behavior, we can also observe its consequences. At sporting events we keep score, tabulate batting averages, etc. In business, we keep production figures and balance sheets. Thus, motivation is not just a theory. It is a reality that we can see, whether we are managing others or ourselves.

A second consideration is the type of behavior we are targeting in others and ourselves. Recently, an interesting literature has emerged on "flow states." Flow states are episodes of behavior that are seemingly unconscious, absorbing, reinforcing, and timeless. Well-publicized examples include long distance runners getting into "the zone", artists and writers in the process of creating where they experience timelessness, selflessness, and total immersion in their work, and surgeons completely absorbed by their tasks in the operating room. Less well publicized experiences which we have all encountered include having a day in which everything seems to go perfectly, an engaging conversation at a cocktail party, playing video games, and reading a book that we enjoy thoroughly. The question is "How do we get to these seemingly effortless and enjoyable motivated states?" From the context of our theory, they are the culmination of understanding our external environment and our internal strengths and weaknesses and then setting challenging goals, which require concentrated effort in order to succeed. Thus, the theorists who have studied flow states contend that those individuals who experience them most frequently are the ones who are able to place themselves on the edge of success and failure so that all their concentration is needed to succeed, resulting in total absorption in the task. Again, from our theoretical perspective, the ability to challenge oneself without being overwhelmed is the result of an unbiased CR style that enables the individual to accurately assess the potential causes of success and failure (i.e., internal/external; stable/unstable). Similarly, effective leaders know both their people (internal) and their environment (external) and are able to work with their people to develop tasks that are challenging but not overwhelming.

Outcomes

Reinforcement is the last component of our model. As B.F. Skinner noted long ago, people repeat behavior when it is reinforced. When people have effective CR styles they select goals that they are likely to achieve and that are likely to be reinforced. In fact, it can easily be argued that the objective of CR is to figure out our world so that we can optimize our reinforcement.

As a result of my consulting experiences, I have come to conclude that nowhere are biases as prevalent as in the area of reinforcement, particularly when it comes to leaders understanding the things that are reinforcing for their employees. A basic maxim of reinforcement is that behavior that is reinforced increases whereas behavior that is punished decreases. Therefore, whenever our employees or we are engaging in inappropriate behavior, it must be more reinforcing than punishing. Similarly, whenever they or we fail to engage in appropriate behaviors, it is because the balance of consequences (total reinforcement and punishment) is or is perceived to be negative. Even though we all understand these principles, bias results in tremendous misunderstandings by both individuals and their leaders.

One of the classic cases of misunderstanding was perpetrated by one of my former employers. In this case they were trying to increase attendance in a dirty, low paying, and punishing work environment. They offered $5 a day for every day a person was in attendance for up to one month, provided that the employees did not have any absences for at least thirty days. Thus, employees could earn up to $150. The program was a dismal failure. Those employees who did not have attendance problems were the ones who collected. Those who had attendance problems could never string the 30 days of consecutive attendance together to start collecting their $5 a day. Instead, those employees with poor attendance purposely stayed home at least three days so that they could collect their sick pay, which far exceeded the measly $5 per day pay-off. What went wrong? The managers failed to consider the balance of consequences for many employees which included abusive supervisors, dirty and hot working conditions, boring jobs, the lack of any consequences for being absent (nobody was ever fired because employees were so hard to replace), and a very liberal sick pay policy. The managers were biased in that they could only see what was reinforcing for themselves and the company. When the senior level managers analyzed their absenteeism problems, they made all external attributions, blaming the employees and failing to see their own policies (i. e., internal) and working conditions as part of the problem.

Several biases appear to come into play when managers and leaders develop reinforcement systems. First, the self-serving bias suggests that leaders and managers will not be motivated to reward employees for success since they want to take the credit for themselves. On the other hand, both the self-serving and actor-observer biases work in the same direction when employees fail, making it likely that they will blame employees for failures. Considering how these biases work, it is not surprising that many work environments appear to rely more on negative (punishment) rather than positive (reinforcement) control.

The notion of hedonic relevance is also important in designing reward systems. Again, this bias suggests that people see their environments in terms of their own rewards and punishments, and often fail to see the perspective from the other people's viewpoints. In working with managers, I am convinced that this is one of the most important biases that must be overcome. More specifically, in sessions where I have worked with managers to help them reduce problem behaviors such as absenteeism and shrinkage (theft), I consistently found it difficult to get the managers to provide an objective list of the employees' rewards and punishments *from the employees' perspectives*. Thus, when managers are asked to list the consequences of absenteeism for an employee, they almost always tell you about the negative consequences of absenteeism *for the organization*. Therefore, a large part of designing effective organizational systems is the ability to objectively recognize the employees' consequences so that you can design systems in which the employees perceive that they are empowered by a stable environment and that they are in control (internal attribution) of their consequences.

CHALLENGES IN THE APPLICATION OF THE MODEL

Most of us will agree that the model is straightforward and unambiguous. As a result, we are tempted to conclude that the application is quite simple. Nothing could be further from the truth. There are a number of reasons why the application of the model is challenging. Most of the reasons relate to the nature of our social and work environments.

Throughout this book, we have relied heavily on examples from sports because the examples are clear and unambiguous. In sports the goals are straightforward: winning the immediate game and, eventually, the championship. The rules are unambiguous, stated in writing, and enforced by a referee. The job descriptions and attributes of the job candidates (height, speed, strength) are well established. Most importantly, the players are highly motivated by the rewards of the game and either volunteer to play in the amateur ranks or are paid handsomely as professionals. Thus, the nature of the environment of sports is as close to ideal as can be imagined and it may be argued that it is easier to apply the principles in these environments.

In the "real world", things are oftentimes much more ambiguous. Goals are unclear, especially in governments and whenever there are multiple stakeholders. In education, for example, it is unclear whether the goals of future employers, legislators, donors, taxpayers, the students, or faculty should take precedence. As a result of unclear goals, performance measures are uncertain. Consequently, it is not clear which measure we should rely on: cost per student, employer satisfaction, student satisfaction, revenue generated by contracts and grants, or academic achievements. In addition, for complex organizations, the environments are constantly changing. Economic and social conditions change and it is often unclear how these changes will affect an organization and how an organization's goals and priorities should change. Because environments, goals, and standards are unclear, there is also ambiguity in the selection criteria for new members as well as for promotions. Thus, the complexity of most modern organizations makes it difficult to diagnose the environment (i.e., causal reasoning) and identify the right goals, hire the right people, reward the right behaviors, and know the probabilities of success for the goals that are selected. Thus, although sports provide a more straightforward setting to demonstrate how principles of motivation work, most of us are faced with environments that are much more uncertain and ambiguous.

Although many of our environments are challenging, these challenges do not negate the validity of our theory. The challenges simply make it more difficult to apply the principles and, sometimes, we lose sight of the principles because of the confusion caused by the complexity of our environments. Thus, one of the major jobs of a leader is to work with the various stakeholders of an organization to try to reach consensus on goals and constantly refer back to the goals as the selection, reward systems, and activities of the organization are implemented. Even though athletic environments appear to be less complex than many work environments, it is important to note that coaches spend significant amounts of time working with administrators, boosters, student athletes, and parents to clarify goals and try to remove ambiguity. Moreover, when controversy does surface in athletics, it is often the result of ambiguity of some kind (e.g., recruiting violations, judgment calls by officials, and the moral versus athletic mission of the institution). Thus, a major task of leaders is to lead their troops through the ambiguity, set agreed-upon goals, and have the courage to develop and administer a reward system that is consistent with the agreed-upon goals. This appears to be exactly what Jack Welch did during his tenure with GE.

Fully explaining the process of teambuilding and strategic planning is beyond the scope of this book. Nonetheless, from the context of CR theory, it is clear that the process of defining the mission and goals of an organization goes more smoothly when all stakeholders (including managers and employees) adopt an unbiased CR style and understand the biases that other stakeholders are likely to exhibit. Moreover, it aids the process greatly when all members trust and respect the integrity of each other. I firmly believe that the moral principles and integrity that both coaches Bowden and Martin have been able to communicate to their players and to the public goes a long way toward alleviating the biases that are likely to occur when the stakes are high and conditions are ambiguous. Thus, trust and faith in the integrity of leaders may be the most important tools they have in alleviating the negative effects of destructive CR styles.

DEFINITIONS

1. *Expectancy*—the probability that one can produce the behaviors required for success as well as the probability that the behaviors will result in the desired rewards.
2. *Flow states*—episodes of behavior that are seemingly unconscious, absorbing, reinforcing, and timeless.

KEY POINTS

1. Individuals who perform at optimal levels are able to objectively analyze their environments and set realistic goals so that they are able to generate the behaviors that they need to be successful.

2. Accomplished investors, contractors, lawyers, and athletes are all able to estimate the likelihood of their successes at the various projects they elect to undertake.

3. The results of the research on goal setting are clear: 1.) people who set goals outperform people who don't set goals; 2.) specific goals result in higher levels of performance than general goals; and 3.) challenging goals result in higher levels of performance than easy goals.

4. The individuals who experience flow states most frequently are those who are able to place themselves on the edge of success so that all their concentration is needed, resulting in total absorption in the task.

5. A large part of designing effective organizational systems is the ability to objectively recognize the employees' consequences and to design systems in which the employees perceive that they are empowered by a stable environment where they are in control (internal attribution) of their consequences.

6. Trust and faith in the integrity of leaders may be the most important tools they have in alleviating the negative effects of destructive CR styles.

CHAPTER XV

HOT TOPICS AND APPLICATIONS

The purpose of this chapter is to relate CR theory and our general model of motivation to the most recent buzzwords and to address contemporary issues like aggression in the workplace, cross-cultural management, and emotional intelligence.

EMPOWERMENT

Both the popular press and academics have devoted considerable attention to the notion of empowering employees. Essentially, the notion of empowerment is giving employees the resources and support that they need to perceive that they are in control of their work environments and their rewards. Within the context of CR theory, employees who are empowered are optimistic employees who believe that their internal and stable attributes (e.g., abilities) and their internal and unstable characteristics (i.e., their efforts) control the causes of their rewards in their work environments. In order to facilitate optimistic perceptions, leaders must structure environments that provide employees the opportunities to achieve higher levels of rewards when they exert more effort or demonstrate superior ability. Such an environment challenges employees to demonstrate their abilities and put forth the effort necessary to excel.

As we discussed in Chapter Five, learned helplessness is the other side of the empowerment coin. Employees who are learned helpless are pessimistic and believe that their failures are due to their own internal and stable attributes such as a lack of ability and that their successes are due to unstable and external causes such as chance and luck. Obviously, leaders can counteract this type of CR pattern by structuring environments so the employees are empowered, as suggested in the paragraph above.

The research that my colleagues and I have conducted documents these notions. In one study, we identified people who were learned helpless versus empowered through standard questionnaire procedures. Then based on the questionnaire results, we divided the sample into two groups: learned helpless and empowered. After that we interviewed the employees without knowing their CR classifications and asked them about their most recent successes and failures. Sure enough, the learned helpless individuals made pessimistic attributions for their failures whereas the empowered people were less pessimistic. On the other hand, the empowered group demonstrated more optimistic attributions for success while the learned helpless group was more prone toward pessimistic attributions for success. In approximately 90% of the cases, based on our impressions from the interviews, we were able to guess the CR style of the interviewees. These findings were important because they demonstrated that people who are diagnosed as empowered and learned helpless via questionnaire instruments actually display the thought processes associated with their categorizations when we talk to them. Likewise, the findings demonstrate that, with experience, it is possible to ascertain whether or not a person is biased toward empowerment or helplessness during interviews and conversations.

ELITE PERFORMANCE

There is a group of researchers in psychology that has been devoted to explaining elite performance. Included in these studies have been Olympic athletes, concert pianists, opera singers, scientists, academic researchers, writers, chess players, and professional athletes including golfers, hockey, and baseball players. In November of 1996 I was invited to a symposia that this group held at Florida State University and I was privileged to sit next to Herb Simon, who had been awarded a Nobel Prize for his work on decision-making. Although a wide constellation of factors affecting elite performance was discussed, there appeared to be consensus on only one factor that separated the elite from the average performers: the amount of disciplined practice. The data showed that in comparing the careers of the elite performers with their contemporaries, there was almost always a marked difference in the time spent in disciplined practice. Thus, for example, although two Olympic gymnasts may have the same apparent skills and talents at sixteen years of age, the difference between the ones who become Olympians and the others is best explained by the amount of practice time. Data showing the bifurcation of practice time between those who became elite performers and those who failed to advance were quite impressive. After discussing these data with Herb Simon, I asked him if he believed that my son could become outstanding at virtually whatever he wanted if he practiced enough. He said yes.

There are some striking examples of the results that are possible with disciplined practice. Today, almost all Olympic-class gymnasts start at a very early age, both in this country and in the former Soviet Union as well as China. Many of us can still remember seeing Tiger Woods on Johnny Carson at a very early age. Similarly, Jennifer Capriati and the Williams sisters were all groomed intensively and at very early ages to become tennis stars. Many pro quarterbacks were groomed at an early age by their fathers, including Dan Marino, Brett Favre, and Brian Griese. Thus, some very smart people and the evidence point to the importance of disciplined practice and support the old saying, "Jack of all trades and master of none." The clear message from this research is that elite performers are single-minded individuals who focus their efforts.

Despite the data and evidence supporting the "disciplined practice" explanation of elite performance, there are still many questions that remain to be answered. It seems obvious that ability must play a role and also that motivation must be involved. Thus, for example, it may be that people with less talent are simply unwilling to commit themselves to disciplined practice because they do not see the results of their efforts. Similarly, those who devote themselves to disciplined practice may do so because they believe that they have the ability (attribution) to be successful if they devote themselves to disciplined practice. In addition, there are also cultures that support disciplined practice. Thus, it does not appear to be an accident that many NBA players come from a particular section of Philadelphia where basketball is king.

Although there does not appear to be any simple one-dimensional explanation for elite performance, you may have guessed by now that CR has a role. My own belief is that the individuals who become elite performers make internal stable and unstable attributions regarding their potential for success. In other words, they believe that they have the ability (internal and stable) but that they have to work hard (internal and unstable) in order to succeed. Those who believe that their successes are a function of hard work and ability will be motivated to engage in the disciplined practice necessary to achieve their potential. From a coaching and management standpoint, encouraging athletes and employees to become elite performers or to maintain elite performance means constant reassurances that they have the talent but not enough to excel unless they commit themselves to the hard work of disciplined practice.

DYSFUNCTIONAL BEHAVIOR

There is mounting conceptual and empirical support that attributions and CR styles are closely related to dysfunctional employee behaviors such as violence, dishonesty, volitional absenteeism, and drug and alcohol abuse. As illustrated in Figure 15.1, dysfunctional behavior can be classified as self-destructive or retaliatory. Counterproductive self-destructive behaviors such as alcoholism, drug abuse, and depression are usually the result of guilt and shame brought on by the internal and stable attributions that lead to learned helplessness. On the other hand, when people engage in counterproductive retaliatory behaviors, they usually experience anger and frustration because they believe that their failures are caused by external and stable causes such as unfair co-workers or supervisors. Thus, for example, we have empirically demonstrated that employees who display hostile CR styles (i.e., attributed their failures to the external and stable actions of others) were much more likely than others to display tendencies toward aggression in the workplace. Much of the current academic and psychological literature stresses environmental factors such as stressful working conditions as a major causal factor when employees "go postal." However, it is important to note that many other employees also experience these same objective conditions without becoming violent. Research is now beginning to demonstrate that although environmental factors certainly play a role in precipitating incidents of aggression and violence, CR styles play a crucial role in differentiating those who are likely to respond with violence and aggression.

Recognizing these CR styles can be an important step in designing strategies to avoid the negative effects of counterproductive behaviors. As suggested by the relations depicted in Figure 15.1, counseling for self-destructive behaviors should usually be oriented towards more optimistic CR (i.e., internal and stable attributions) for success. On the other hand, interventions for managing retaliatory behaviors would attempt to move the individuals toward external and unstable attributions for failure (e.g., the economy) and to more recognition of personal responsibility (i.e., internal attributions for negative events). Thus, even though a slight bias toward optimistic attribution styles appears to be healthy, accentuated optimistic biases that fail to recognize legitimate personal responsibility for failure should be discouraged. In addition, active public relations programs emphasizing the external and unstable causes (e.g., the economy) for negative outcomes (e.g., downsizing) can influence individuals who are negatively affected to make attributions that are unlikely to lead to retaliatory behaviors.

Hot Topics and Applications

Situational Variables
- Leadership Style
- Inflexible Policies
- Reward Systems
- Competitive Environment
- Rules & Procedures
- Economic Conditions
- Adverse Working Conditions
- Nature of Task
- Home Life

Individual Differences
- Attribution Style
- Negative Affectivity
- Emotional Stability
- Integrity
- Gender
- Core Self-Evaluation
  —Nonneurotocism
  —Locus of Control
  —Self-Esteem
  —Generalized Self-Efficacy

Causal Reasoning

Perceptions of Disequilibria

Attributions
internal/stable
external/stable

Emotions

Guilt/Shame

Anger and Frustration

Counterproductive Behavior

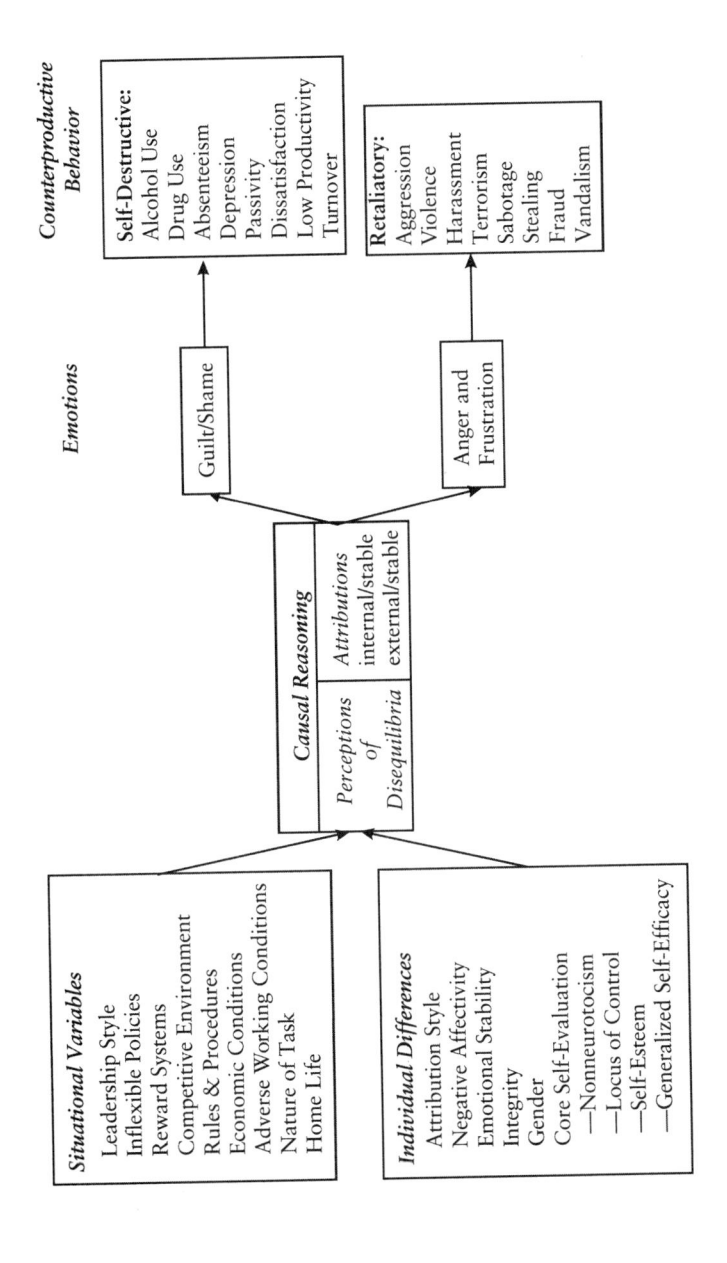

Self-Destructive:
Alcohol Use
Drug Use
Absenteeism
Depression
Passivity
Dissatisfaction
Low Productivity
Turnover

Retaliatory:
Aggression
Violence
Harassment
Terrorism
Sabotage
Stealing
Fraud
Vandalism

FIGURE 15.1. A CR Model of Counterproductive Behavior

SELF-ESTEEM AND SELF-EFFICACY

Self-esteem is an overall feeling of self-worth and positive regard whereas self-efficacy is a measure of a person's confidence that he or she will succeed at a particular task. The relationship between self-esteem and self-efficacy is a mirror of the relationship between attributions and CR style. As we discussed earlier, attributions are causal explanations whereas CR style is a person's tendency to make certain types of attributions. From the perspective of CR theory, self-efficacy is the result of causal attributions relating to the likelihood of success at a particular task (e.g., a person believes she will do well in a sales presentation because of the internal and stable attribution that she is a good public speaker). On the other hand, high self-esteem is the result of a generally optimistic CR style whereas low self-esteem is the result of a pessimistic attribution style.

Research has demonstrated that, all other things being equal, individuals with high self-esteem generally outperform those with low self-esteem, but not always. From a common sense standpoint, we all know that simply thinking you are good does not make you good. It may make you try harder and be more willing to try something, but you still have to make the effort and have the talent, ability, and environment that make success possible. That is where self-efficacy enters into the picture. Within the context of CR theory, self-efficacy is the result of the causal analysis (i.e., attributions) of the probabilities of success in the environment. When individuals believe that they have the abilities (internal/stable) and resources (external stable) they need, they are confident that their efforts will be successful and express high self-efficacy. On the other hand when individuals doubt their abilities and resources, they express low self-efficacy.

Why are self-esteem and self-efficacy important? At first, self-esteem received the most attention when it was found that overall self-concept was related to general life success and well-being. Educators then placed an emphasis on self-esteem, but the results were disappointing. Student achievement did not necessarily follow increases in self-esteem. With further analysis, self-efficacy emerged as the new "call to arms" in education. And the results have been and are certainly encouraging. Sophisticated analyses of studies using a variety of variables to predict successful performance document that self-efficacy is one of the strongest predictors of performance, in both academic and business settings. These findings are not surprising within the context of CR theory. Based on CR theory, we would expect that, over time, most people develop a reasonable knowledge of their environments and their own capabilities. Thus, they have a good idea of the causes of success. As a result, we should not be surprised that when people expect to succeed (i.e., have high self-efficacy), it is highly probable that they do succeed. Most importantly, however, self-efficacy estimates are not the cause of success and it is unlikely that we can make appreciable increases in performance by convincing people to fool themselves and make overly optimistic efficacy estimates (i.e., attributions) for success. On the other hand, efficacy estimates can be very important, particularly when they are unrealistically low or high. These unrealistic estimates suggest that the individuals may be misperceiving their environments or their own capabilities. In these types of cases, interventions (e.g., counseling or raising awareness) designed to help individuals make more realistic attributions for their performance may be helpful.

IMPRESSION MANAGEMENT

Another topic that has received considerable recent attention is the notion of impression management, which includes the notions of self-monitoring and political behavior. The basic thesis of this body of work is that people, and leaders in particular, engage in behavior designed to create intended impressions in others. Examples of these types of behaviors include intimidation, supplication, accounts, explanations, apologies, and denigrating others. Those individuals who demonstrate high frequencies of impression management behaviors are high self-monitors whereas low self-monitors engage in impression management with far less frequency. Although these behaviors often have destructive political motives, they can also have positive consequences. For example, an employee who has a very poor performance on a job as a result of a lack of resources can improve both his or her evaluation and the potential for organizational success by explaining to the manager (i.e., giving an account) the types of resources that are required to do the job right. Such an explanation could shift the manager's CR from an internal to an external attribution for the employee's poor performance. Thus, impression management attempts can be framed and interpreted from a CR perspective. Knowing the exact nature of the attribution you or someone else is attempting to create can make the process more manageable and understandable.

Research on impression management has fairly consistently demonstrated that high self-monitors are perceived to be more effective leaders than others and that they are selected for positions of leadership more often that others. In my experience, these findings are sometimes surprising to low self-monitors because they see impression management behaviors as false and duplicitous. Another way of perceiving such behaviors is that they are a tool that enables us to reduce biased CR in others by presenting more accurate representations of events. In addition, genuine attempts at impression management also show that you care about the impressions you make, demonstrating sensitivity and awareness. On the other hand, research has also demonstrated that when people perceive purposeful and intentional impression management attempts that are designed to manipulate the target for the benefit of the actor, the attempts backfire. Like so many things in life, the morality of the use of these techniques is similar to the use of any other tool that can create both good and harm. The morality depends on the purpose and intent of the behaviors.

EMOTIONAL INTELLIGENCE

Emotional intelligence is the latest buzzword and is simply the recognition that there are other kinds of smarts besides the kind that are associated with success in school. Examples of emotional intelligence are: knowing when getting mad can result in a productive versus unproductive reaction by an employee; reading your audience and knowing what to say next (an example of self-monitoring); leaders who know how and when to be human relations or task oriented in their transactions; and recognizing when a colleague is receptive versus not receptive to feedback.

The concept of different types of intelligences is not new and was explored extensively in the 1930's, but no one was ever really successful in measuring other global intelligences and predicting a very wide range of meaningful behavior with these alternative measurements. On the other hand, IQ was and is a very good measure for predicting success in traditional schools.

In order to understand emotional intelligence, it is helpful to understand IQ tests and how and why they have been so useful. The original test was developed by Binet in France to help sort out how to place students when the public education system was initiated. Since the population was mostly rural, the test included questions such as where milk comes from, how do you make butter, and so forth. Binet found that children's everyday knowledge about their world was a good way to sort students. Those who scored higher and knew more were put in advanced grades while those who scored low were put into lower grades.

The success of the French system encouraged educators from Stanford in the United States to try using the same tests. They were translated and administered but appeared to be confusing to the students and did not prove to be as predictive here as they were in France. After closely looking at the items, it was found that many were culturally biased, asking for answers that French children but not children in the U.S. would be likely to know. The items were changed and eventually the Stanford-Binet test was the end result. The effectiveness of the test was measured by how well the test predicted school performance and it did quite well. After that, the Stanford-Binet was used as the yardstick to which virtually every intelligence test was compared.

In addition to school performance, IQ tests have also proved to be useful, but not as powerful, in predicting a wide range of behaviors such as career success, financial status, and general health. However, the markedly lower power of the predictions for these other types of behavioral domains made it patently clear that other factors are also important in predicting successful behaviors. Thus, in the last twenty years, academics and researchers have renewed the exploration of multiple intelligences including social and emotional intelligence.

The problem with the construct of emotional intelligence is that there are so many different behaviors and nuances of emotional intelligence. As a result, it has been extremely difficult to find a single measure that is predictive of the wide and varied range of behaviors that we are concerned with in work settings. Thus, for example, the ability to reserve judgment may be an important behavior for a circuit court judge but may be detrimental to the efficiency of a judge in traffic court. Similarly, the ability to read an audience and entertain the audience may be very important for a CEO but not critical for an accountant or research scientist. Thus, it appears unlikely that researchers will ever agree on a measure of emotional intelligence that is predictive of the wide range of behaviors in which we are interested.

Regardless of agreement among the academic community, from a practical perspective, we all know that that there are intelligences beyond IQ that are important for success, even in academia. While I have been at Florida State I have been very active in working with our doctoral program and recruiting top-level students. Over the years it has become clear that, while standardized tests (in this case, the GMAT) are predictive of academic performance, there are other factors that are equally important which include prior performance, the ability to communicate (teaching and presentation skills), the candidates' academic and career objectives, and the desire to do research and contribute to the body of knowledge in the management area. While one can never really know exactly how a student will turn out, it is nonetheless clear that factors other than the GMAT are critically important in determining who will be the high performers.

At least one of those factors appears to be an objective and perhaps even hypercritical CR style. More specifically, up to the point of graduate programs, most educational programs treat students as reservoirs, requiring them to learn and regurgitate, but not develop, facts and information. In a doctoral program, students are challenged to develop and create research. The process of creating requires very objective assessments of both their environments and themselves. When papers are submitted for publication, the review process is often brutal. The feedback is often accurate but many times is off-track because the reviewers fail to fully comprehend the author's point of view. Sometimes the author is wrong, sometimes the author simply needs to explain his or her position better, and sometimes the reviewers are wrong. Nevertheless, there is always something wrong and papers are virtually never accepted in top-level journals until the authors address the reviewers' reservations. Thus, being successful in this process requires being able to objectively view your own work as well as the works of others and objectively identify both the problems and merits of the work. Criticisms of the work can be the result of many factors including the author's failure to write clearly, the reviewer's lack of ability to understand the theory, biased reviewers protecting their turf, lack of substantiating data, and the selection of an ambiguous, poorly defined, or trivial topic. Recognizing where the problems with the paper lie (i.e., internal or external) and whether or not they can be fixed (stable or unstable) is a type of intelligence that we are only learning to measure.

Thus it appears that CR is an important component of emotional and social intelligence. CR provides a baseline for giving and receiving feedback, knowing when you are right or wrong (and whether you should continue fighting or give in), recognizing opportunities and challenges, solving interpersonal problems, and resolving and avoiding conflict. While CR is certainly not the only factor involved in emotional intelligence, it is clear that objective CR (i.e., understanding yourself and your environment) is a central factor in the constellation of factors that we call emotional intelligence.

CROSS-CULTURAL MANAGEMENT

CR theory also helps to explain some of the differences in cultural orientations. In general, the research has demonstrated that many Pacific Rim and Spanish-speaking cultures are much more collectivistic and therefore much more likely to make external attributions for both success and failure than traditional western cultures. Although the research in this area is still in an exploratory phase, the findings suggest that differences in CR styles may help to explain the failure of many expatriate managers to complete their overseas assignments. More specifically, the tendency in some cultures to be biased toward external attributions for failure experiences exacerbates the effects of both the self-serving and actor-observer biases between leaders and subordinates, particularly under conditions of failure. Thus, as illustrated earlier in Tables 9.1 and 9.2, most of the CR biases influence leaders to blame members for failures whereas these same biases influence members to blame external causes (oftentimes leaders) for their failures. The cross-cultural research on CR styles indicates that these differences may be even more accentuated when leaders and members are from different cultures.

In conclusion, the research and theory support the notion that CR styles are related to the conflicts that have been documented between expatriate leaders and their host country members. In order to counteract the effects of these biases, several researchers and consultants have developed or are in the process of developing programs to help expatriate managers manage cross-cultural CR biases with the intent of reducing the stress and conflict often associated with expatriate assignments. The information contained in Chapter Ten provides a general description of the types of strategies that can be applied to alleviate biases between cultures through CR training programs.

PERFORMANCE APPRAISALS

Both leaders and members can consider performance appraisal an exercise in CR as they try to search for and evaluate the causes of the member's performance. Attention to attribution errors is particularly critical in the appraisal process. Recent trends in performance appraisal such as the 360-degree appraisal process can be understood as an attempt to eliminate CR biases by the use of multiple perspectives. This process, of course, is consistent with the notion of multiple raters that was suggested in Chapter Ten as a way of overcoming the negative effects of CR biases. In addition, it would seem that more explicit causal appraisals during the performance appraisal process would yield still more effective and useful results. This can be a difficult option for line managers whose own self-serving biases mitigate against the recognition that they play some role in the failures of their employees.

SELECTION PROCESSES

As stressed throughout this book, because effective leaders use CR to diagnose and understand their environments, they know the needs of the organization and the types of characteristics needed in individuals to fulfill the vacuum left by vacant positions.

Questionnaires, interviews, references, and histories of past performance and experiences provide the information necessary to determine if a person is a good fit for the organization. In addition, our research on CR demonstrates that oftentimes individuals reveal their CR styles during interviews where they are asked to describe and account for their prior successes and failures. It would seem that, in most cases, one would want employees who demonstrate reasonably unbiased CR styles. In addition, recent research on integrity testing has found that these tests can be fairly predictive of counterproductive behaviors such as stealing. Moreover, many of the items on these tests appear to tap causal reasoning, asking subjects whether or not stealing can be justified as a means of making up for unfair treatment. Finally, there is evidence that employees who steal tend to have external attribution styles. Thus, it appears that CR can be an important job-related criterion for selection processes.

CHARISMATIC AND TRANSFORMATIONAL LEADERSHIP

The above section on the limitations of the general motivation model alluded to the notions of charismatic and transformational leadership. By definition, a transformational leader provides and reinforces a vision that redefines the organization so that it is more adaptive, responsive, and effective in a changing environment. Transformational leaders use their charisma to communicate and reinforce their vision. While charismatic and transformational leadership are very similar, there is a distinction. From the perspective of CR theory, charismatic and transformational leaders have the ability to assess their environments, see the possibilities, and create a vision that ties members' needs to the needs of the organization. Transformational leaders make ample use of impression management (and then we call it charisma) to help members see how their objectives meet the personal interests and needs of the members. Within the context of CR theory, charisma is the result of the ability to objectively analyze causation in the environment for both managerial and member outcomes and then to provide the behavior (task or human relations oriented) that is appropriate and needed for the situation. When members see that the leader has a clear vision of where the organization and its people need to go, understands the capabilities and limitations of the individual members, and behaves in a way that takes full advantage of the opportunities of the organization and the skills of the employees, they say that she or he demonstrates charisma. Thus, from the perspective of CR theory, transformational and charismatic leadership behaviors are simply another name for the behaviors of leaders who are effective and efficient in understanding their world and are able to sell their vision to their members as a way to solve both member and organizational problems.

FINAL THOUGHTS

At the beginning, it was stated that this book is an attempt to give a realistic description of the factors that are critical for achieving optimal individual and organizational performance. As promised, the book is not a cookbook and there is no set of 10 simple steps for success. Success is a subjective goal that has multiple meanings depending on whose perspective and biases (including our own) define the objective. Nonetheless, both individuals and organizations set goals and some people are much better at achieving their dreams and organizational goals. While CR is not the whole answer to achieving optimal performance, it is at least a crucial part of the puzzle.

In this book we have taken a look at our own CR styles through the self-assessments and have examined the prototypical style of both optimists and pessimists. We have also taken a good look at the styles of two extremely successful people, coaches Bowden and Martin, concluding that both of these coaches display emotionally intelligent and apparently unbiased CR styles. They see it as it is, tell it like it is, and act accordingly. We considered suggestions for managing our own biases as well as those of others as a way to reduce conflict and channel our energies toward optimal performance as individuals and as members of organizations. Finally, we considered how CR fits within the larger scheme of theories of motivation. While this discussion recognizes that there are many other factors that play a role in motivated behavior, it also demonstrates that CR is a critical part of the motivational puzzle that cannot be ignored if you are pursuing optimal performance. It is my sincerest hope that this book has been helpful to you by describing the crucial role of CR and by providing strategies that can help you achieve optimal performance and facilitate the same level of excellence in others.

DEFINITIONS

Empowerment—providing the resources and support that employees need to perceive that they are in control of their work environments and their rewards.

Self-esteem—a person's overall feeling of self-worth and positive regard.

Self-efficacy—a person's belief that he or she will succeed at a specific task.

Impression Management—the notion that individuals engage in behavior designed to create specific impressions (e.g., power, authority, and trustworthiness) in others.

High Self-Monitors—Individuals who are motivated to read an audience and produce impressions that an audience will judge positively.

Emotional Intelligence—As distinguished from academic intelligence, the ability to read the environment and know how to behave in social situations.

Transformational Leader—a leader that develops and reinforces a vision that redefines the organization so that it is adaptive, responsive, and effective in a changing environment.

Charismatic Leader—a leader that followers strongly identify with and who is perceived to embody the values, vision, and hopes of the followers.

KEY POINTS

1. It is possible to ascertain a person's CR style through interviews and conversations.
2. The amount of disciplined practice appears to be a critical factor that separates elite from average performers.
3. Counterproductive self-destructive behaviors such as alcoholism, drug abuse, and depression are often the result of the guilt and shame brought on by pessimistic internal and stable attributions for failure.
4. Counterproductive retaliatory behaviors such as organizational violence and vandalism are often the result of anger and frustration brought on by the belief that failures are the result of external and stable causes such as unfair co-workers or supervisors.

5. High self-esteem is the result of a generally optimistic CR style whereas low self-esteem is the result of a generally pessimistic attribution style.

6. Research indicates that high self-monitors are perceived to be more effective leaders and are selected for positions of leadership more often than low self-monitors.

7. Impression management attempts often backfire when people perceive that they are designed to manipulate the target for the benefit of the actor.

8. Objective CR (i.e., understanding yourself and your environment) is a central factor in the constellation of factors that we call emotional intelligence.

9. Differences in CR styles may help to explain the failure of many expatriate managers to complete their overseas assignments.

NOTES AND REFERENCES

CHAPTER I: INTRODUCTION

The discussion of Tiger Woods' mindset is contained in S.L. Price, 2000. Tiger Woods. *Sports Illustrated*, 92 (14), April 3, 81-90.

CHAPTER II: SELF-ASSESSMENT

A discussion of the various alternatives and measures for assessing attribution style appears in Kent, R. & Martinko, M. J. 1995. The measurement of attributions in organizational research. In Martinko, M. J.(Ed.). *Attribution theory: An Organizational Perspective*. Delray Beach, FL.: St. Lucie Press. P. 17-34.

    There are a variety of instruments that have been used to assess attribution styles. The following articles describe these instruments or discuss research on these instruments: Kent, R. & Martinko, M. J. 1995. The development and evaluation of a scale to measure organizational attribution style, in Martinko, M.J. (Ed.), *Attribution theory: An Organizational Perspective*. Delray Beach, FL.: St. Lucie Press, p. 53-75; Campbell, C. R., & Martinko, M. J. 1998. An integrative attributional perspective of empowerment and learned helplessness: a multimethod field study. *Journal of Management*, 24(2): 173-200; Moss, S. E., & Martinko, M. J. 1997. The effects of performance attributions and outcome dependence on leader feedback behavior following poor subordinate performance. *Journal of Organizational Behavior*, 19: 259-274; Peterson, C. & Villanova, P. 1988. An expanded attributional style questionnaire, *Journal of Abnormal Psychology*, 97, (1), 87-89; Cutrona, Carolyn E., Russell, Dan, and Jones, R. Dallas. 1985. Cross-situational consistency in causal attributions: does attributional style exist? *Journal of Personality and Social Psychology*, 47, 1043-1058; Anderson, C.A. 1983.The Causal Structure of Situations: The

Notes and References

Generation of Plausible Causal Attributions as a Function of Type of Event Situation. *Journal of Experimental Social Psychology*, 19, 185-203; Peterson, C., Semmel, A., von Beyer, C., Abramson, L., Metalsky, G., & Seligman, M. 1982. The Attribution Style Questionnaire. *Cognitive Therapy and Research*, 6(3): 287-300.

Some of the scales used to measure attribution style assess only dimensions (e.g., internal versus external) while others focus on causal explanations (e.g., ability and effort). There is some debate about the validity of these various methods. The scales developed for this book are intended as a learning tool as well as an assessment instrument. They include both dimensions and causal explanations, so that the respondents can see how dimensions relate to explanations.

Many of the scales ask the respondents to evaluate the dimensions of a single cause. The scales here allow for the assessment of multiple causes. Although there are advantages and disadvantages to both approaches, I believe that the recognition of multiple causes makes the most sense and functions well as a learning tool as well as an assessment instrument.

CHAPTER III. CAUSAL REASONING

Many researchers point to Heider's work as the origin of attribution theory: Heider, F.1958. *The psychology of interpersonal relations*. New York: Wiley. There are number of sources from the psychology literature that describe the foundations and contributions of attribution theory. They include the work of Seligman and his colleagues: Seligman, M. 1991. *Learned Optimism*, New York: Alfred A. Knopf.; Abramson, L. Y., Seligman, M. E.P., Teasdale, John D. 1978. Learned helplessness in humans: critique and reformulation. *Journal of Abnormal Psychology*, 87, 49-74; Seligman, M. and Schulman, P. 1986. Explanatory style as a predictor of productivity and quitting among life insurance agents. *Journal of Personality and Social Psychology*, 50(4), 832-838. The work of Weiner and his colleagues has also made a major contribution to defining the field and describing the role of attributions. Key sources from this body of work include: Weiner, B. 1985. An attributional theory of achievement motivation and emotion. *Psychological Review*, 92: 548-573; Weiner, B. 1986. *An attributional theory of motivation and emotion*, New York: Springer-Verlag; Weiner, B. 1995. Judgments of responsibility: A foundation for a theory of social conduct. New York: Guilford Press; Weiner, B., Graham, S. & Chandler, C. 1982. Pity, Anger, and Guilt: An Attributional Analysis. *Personality and Social Psychology Bulletin*, 8, 226-232; Weiner, B., Russell, D. & Lerman, D. 1978. Affective Consequences of Causal Ascriptions. In J.H. Harvey, W.J. Ickes & R.F. Kidd (Eds.), *New Directions in Attribution Research*, Vol.2, Hillsdale, N.J.: Erlbaum, 59-88. The early work of Kelley was also important to the development of the field: Kelley, H.H. 1973. The process of causal attribution. *American Psychologist*, 28, 107-128.

In the management literature, the following sources are recommended: Martinko, M. J. 1995. The nature and function of attribution theory within the organizational sciences. In M. J. Martinko, (Ed.), *Attribution theory: An Organizational Perspective*, Delray Beach, FL.: St. Lucie Press, pp. 7-16; Martinko, M.J. and Gardner, W.L. 1982. Learned helplessness: An alternative explanation for performance deficits. *Academy of Management Review*, 7(2), 195-204. Reprinted in Davis, K. and Newstrom, J.W. *Organizational Behavior: Readings and Exercises*, Seventh Edition, New York: McGraw-Hill, 1985, 65-80; Martinko, M.J. and Thompson, N. 1998. A synthesis of the Weiner and Kelley attribution models. *Journal of Basic and Applied Psychology*, 20(4), 271-284.

There has been considerable discussion and some disagreement regarding the dimensions of causal explanations. Almost all researchers include the locus of causality (i.e., internal/external) and stability (i.e., stable/unstable) dimensions and many of the references listed above describe or suggest the relationships depicted in Figure 3.1. However, other dimensions such as controllability, globality, and intentionality have also been suggested and discussed. In many cases these dimensions do not appear to be independent of the locus of causality and stability dimensions. Thus, for example, factor analyses show that locus of causality and controllability dimensions are highly correlated and interrelated. The globality and stability dimensions are also highly correlated. Because of these similarities and in the interest of clarity, I have elected to restrict the discussions of attribution styles primarily to the two dimensions that have the most research support: locus of causality and stability. It is also a whole lot easier to describe attribution styles as a function of these two dimensions. Adding an additional dimension would double the number of possible styles, making the discussion and description of attribution styles unwieldy. In addition, because the additional dimensions appear to be intercorrelated with the original dimensions, descriptions of the various styles would become very confusing. Nonetheless, interested readers and researchers may want to consult the suggested readings to get a better understanding of the potential of these other dimensions to add to our knowledge.

CHAPTER IV. THE ARCHETYPAL OPTIMIST

This case is fictitious. It is not based on any specific individual and is told in the first person to add a personality to the concept of the optimist. Any resemblance to any specific person is coincidental.

CHAPTER V. THE PESSIMISTIC CR STYLE

Some references for the early work on learned helplessness are: Overmier, J.B. & Seligman, M. E. P. 1967. Effects of inescapable shock upon subsequent escape and avoidance learning. *Journal of Comparative and Physiological Psychology*, 63, 28-33; Seligman, M.E.P. and Maier, S.F. Failure to escape traumatic shock, *Journal of Experimental Psychology*, 1967, 74, 1-9; Hiroto, D.S. and Seligman, M.E.P., Generality of learned helplessness in man, *Journal of Personality and Social Psychology*, 1975, 31, 311-327; and Abramson, L. Y., Seligman, M. E. P., & Teasdale, J. D. (1978). Learned helplessness in humans: Critique and reformulation. *Journal of Abnormal Psychology*, 87(1), pp. 49-74. Reviews and empirical work on the application of learned helplessness in organizational contexts can be found in: Martinko, M. J. and Gardner, W. L. 1982. Learned helplessness: An alternative explanation for performance deficits, *Academy of Management Review*, Vol. 7(2), pp. 195-204; Martinko, M. J. and Gardner, W. L. 1987. The leader member attribution process. *Academy of Management Review*, 12 (2), pp. 235-249; Campbell, Constance R. & Martinko, Mark J. 1998. An integrative attributional perspective of empowerment and learned helplessness: a multimethod field study. *Journal of Management*, 24(2), 173-200; Seligman, M. and Schulman, P. 1986. Explanatory style as a predictor of productivity and quitting among life insurance agents. *Journal of Personality and Social Psychology*, 50(4),832-838. Henry, J. & Martinko, M. J. 1997. An attributional analysis of the rejection of new information technologies. *Journal of End User Computing*, 9(4), 3-17; Martinko, M. 1981. Breaking the pattern of learned helplessness. *Training*, 18 (8), 110-113; Moss, S. E. & Martinko, M. J. 1997. The effects of performance attributions and outcome dependence on leader feedback behavior following poor subordinate performance. *Journal of Organizational Behavior*, 19, 259-274; Martinko, M. J., Henry, J, and Zmud, R. 1996. Learned Helplessness: A theoretical explication of reactions to information technologies in the workplace. *Behavior and Information Technology*, 15(5), 313-330.

CHAPTER VIII. THE EMOTIONALLY INTELLIGENT CAUSAL REASONING STYLE: BOBBY BOWDEN AND NUMBER 11

The interviews described in this chapter were conducted in the spring of 1997.

CHAPTER IX: PERCEPTUAL BIASES THAT CLOUD CAUSAL REASONING

The following references provide definitions and descriptions of the various types of attribution errors and biases: Jones, E.E. & Nisbett, R.E. 1972. The actor and the observer: Divergent causes of perceptions of behavior. In E. Jones, D. Kanouse, H. Kelley, R. Nisbett, S. Valins, & B.

Weiner (Eds.), *Attribution: Perceiving the causes of behavior.* Morristown, N.J., 1-16; Martinko, M. 1995. Definitions of: attribution and fundamental attribution error. In *The Blackwell Dictionary of Organizational Behavior*, London: Blackwell Publishers, 21-23, 532, 533. Martinko, M.J. 1995. Attribution theory, in Nigel Nicholson (Ed.), The Blackwell Dictionary of Organizational Behavior, London: Blackwell Publishers, 1995, 21-23; Nasby, W., Hayden, B. & DePaulo, B.M. 1979. Attributional Bias Among Aggressive Boys to Interpret Unambiguous Social Stimuli as Displays of Hostility. *Journal of Abnormal Psychology* 89: 459-68; VanOostrum, N. 1997. The effects of hostile attribution on adolescents' aggressive responses to social situations. *Canadian Journal of School Psychology*, 13(1), 48-59; Martinko, M. J. & Gardner, W.L. (1982). Learned helplessness: An alternative explanation for performance deficits. *Academy of Management Review*, 7(2), 195-204.

The following articles describe the impact of attribution errors on leader-member relations: Martinko, M. & Gardner, W. 1987. The leader member attribution process, *Academy of Management Review*, 12 (2), 235-249; Green, S. & Mitchell, T. 1979. Attributional processes of leaders in leader-member interactions, *Organizational Behavior and Human Performance*, 23, 429-458; Moss, S. E. & Martinko, M. J. 1997. The effects of performance attributions and outcome dependence on leader feedback behavior following poor subordinate performance. *Journal of Organizational Behavior*, 19, 259-274. Martinko, M. J. (2000). Basic motivation. In *Organizational Behavior:* Primis Edition, Fred Luthans (Ed.), New York: McGraw-Hill; Mitchell, T.R. and Wood, R.E. 1980. Supervisor's Responses to Subordinate Poor Performance: A Test of an Attributional Model. *Organizational Behavior and Human Performance*, 23, 429-458.

CHAPTER X. TOWARD AN EMOTIONALLY INTELLIGENT CAUSAL REASONING STYLE: OVERCOMING THE EFFECTS OF CR BIASES

The classic reference on negotiating is: Fisher, R. & Ury, R. 1981. *Getting to Yes*. Penguin Books.

The original research on the actor-observer bias (Jones, E.E. & Nisbett, R.E. 1972. The actor and the observer: Divergent causes of perceptions of behavior. In E. Jones, D. Kanouse, H. Kelley, R. Nisbett, S. Valins, & B. Weiner (Eds.), *Attribution: Perceiving the causes of behavior*. Morristown, N.J., 1-16) demonstrates that increasing physical proximity and empathy decreases actor-observer biases.

Other articles describing attributional biases, their effects, and interventions for overcoming attributional biases include: Martinko, M. J. & Gardner, W. L. 1982. Learned helplessness: An alternative explanation for performance deficits. *Academy of Management Review*, 7(2), 195-204; Martinko, M. J. & Gardner, W. L. 1987. The leader-member attribution process. *Academy of Management Review*, 12(2), 235-249; Martinko, M.

J., Henry, J., and Zmud, R. 1996. Learned Helplessness: A theoretical explication of reactions to information technologies in the workplace. *Behavior and Information Technology*, 15(5), 313-330; Martinko, M. J. & Douglas, S. C. 1999. Culture and expatriate failure: An attributional explication. *The International Journal of Organizational Analysis*, 7(3), 266-294.

A number of articles have demonstrated and discussed the relationship between attributions, impression management behaviors, and their effects on leader behavior. They include: Gardner, W. L., and Martinko, M. J. 1988. Impression management in Organizations. *Journal of Management*, 14(2), 321-338. Gardner, W. L., and Martinko, M. J. 1988. Impression Management: An Observational Study Linking Audience Characteristics with Verbal Self-Presentations. *Academy of Management Journal*, 31 (1), 42-65; Martinko, Mark J. 1991. Future Directions: Towards a Model for Applying Impression Management Strategies in the Workplace. In Giacalone, R. and Rosenfeld, P., Editors. *Applied Impression Management: How Image Making Affects Managerial Decisions*. Sage Publications, 259-277.

Some references for teambuilding include: Katzenbach, J.R. & Smith, D. K. 1993. *The wisdom of teams: Creating the high performance organization*, Boston, MA.: Harvard Business School Press; Dyer, W.G. 1977. *Team Building: Issues and alternatives*, Reading, MA: Addison-Wesley; Sundstrom, E., DeMeuse, K.P., & Futrell, D. 1990. Work teams: Applications and effectiveness, *American Psychologist*, 45, 120-133.

CHAPTER XI. INTERPRETING THE SELF-TEST: PART II

The research on attribution styles has primarily focused on intrapersonal rather than interpersonal (social) styles. Although the early work of Kelley and his colleagues addresses the issue of observer attributions and later research looks at how attributions about the behaviors of others affect observers' (e. g., leaders') behaviors, there has been little discussion of social attribution *styles*. One exception is the literature on aggression that discusses the notion of hostile attribution biases (e.g., Nasby, W., Hayden, B. & DePaulo, B.M. 1979. Attributional Bias Among Aggressive Boys to Interpret Unambiguous Social Stimuli as Displays of Hostility. *Journal of Abnormal Psychology*, 89: 459-68. Martinko, M. J, & Zellars, K. L. 1998. Toward a theory of workplace violence: A cognitive appraisal perspective. In Griffin, R. W., O'Leary-Kelly, A. & J. M. Collins, J.M. editors. *Dysfunctional behavior in organizations: Violent and deviant behavior*. Stanford, CT: JAI Press, 1-42; Dodge, K.A. 1987. Hostile attribution biases among aggressive boys are exacerbated under conditions of threats to the self. *Child Development*, 57(1): 213-224; Douglas, S. C. & Martinko, M. J. 2001. Exploring the role of individual differences in the prediction of workplace aggression. *Journal of Applied Psychology.*86(4), 547-559). Another exception is our own work which has described the theoretical foundations for the notion of observer attribution styles and documented the existence of these styles in work settings: Thomson, N. & Martinko, M. Observer attribution style: A conceptual model. Paper presented at the Annual Meeting of the Academy of Management, 1995; Thomson, N. and Martinko, M. 1998. Observer attribution style: An empirical analysis of the cross-situational stability of observer attributions. In Barr, S. (Ed.), *Southern Management Association Proceedings*, 86-89; and Martinko, M. J. & Thompson, Neal. 1998. A synthesis of the Weiner and Kelley attribution models. *Journal of Basic and Applied Psychology*, 20(4), 271-284.

CHAPTER XIII. MANAGING INTERPERSONAL CR STYLES

The suggestions for managing helplessness come from four primary sources: Martinko, M. 1981. Breaking the pattern of learned helplessness. *Training*, 18(8), 110-113; Martinko, M. J. & Gardner, W. L. 1982. Learned helplessness: An alternative explanation for performance deficits. *Academy of Management Review*, 7(2), 195-204; Martinko, M. J., Henry, John, and Zmud, R. 1996. Learned Helplessness: A theoretical explication of reactions to information technologies in the workplace. *Behavior and Information Technology*, 15(5), 313-330; and Martinko, M. J. and Douglas, S. C. 1999. Culture and expatriate failure: An attributional explication. *The International Journal of Organizational Analysis*, 7(3), 266-294.

CHAPTER XIV. THE BIG PICTURE

Some of the research and theory supporting the basic motivation paradigm includes: Bandura, A. 1977. *Social learning theory*. Englewood Cliffs, N.J.: Prentice-Hall; Bandura, A.1988. Self-regulation of motivation and action through goal systems. In V. Hamilton, G. H. Bower, & N. H. Frijda, (Eds.), *Cognitive Perspectives on Emotion and Motivation*. Dordrecht, Netherlands: Kluwer Academic Publishers; Davis, T. & Luthans, F. 1980. A social learning approach to organizational behavior. *Academy of Management Review*, 281-290; Weiner, B. 1985. An attributional theory of achievement motivation and emotion. *Psychology Review*, 92: 548-573; Skinner, B. F. 1957. *Verbal behavior*. New York: Appleton-Century-Crofts; and Vroom, V. H. 1964. *Work and Motivation*. New York: John Wiley.

References and a discussion of the research supporting the importance of goal setting can be found in Locke, E. A. & Latham, G. P. 1990. *A Theory of Goal Setting and Task Performance*. Prentice Hall: Englewood Cliffs, N.J.

References describing reinforcement theory and interventions include: Luthans, F. & Kreitner, R. 1985. *Organizational Behavior Modification and Beyond,* Scott Forseman: Glenview, Illinois; Luthans, F. &

Martinko, M. J. 1978. *The Power of Positive Reinforcement*, McGraw-Hill Book Company; Martinko, Mark J., Casey, William, and Fadil, Paul. 2001. An operant approach to sales management. In C. Merle Johnson, Redmon, William K., and Mawhinney, Thomas C. (Ed.). *Handbook of Organizational Performance: Behavior Analysis and Management*. Hayworth Press, 327-344.

CHAPTER XV. HOT TOPICS AND APPLICATIONS

The reference for the study that examined the relationships between attributions and empowerment is: Campbell, C. R. and Martinko, M. J. 1998. An integrative attributional perspective of empowerment and learned helplessness: a multimethod field study. *Journal of Management*, 24(2), 173-200.

The single best source regarding the psychology of expert performance is: Ericsson, K. A. (Ed.). 1996. *The road to excellence: The acquisition of expert performance in the arts and sciences sports and games*. Mahwah, N.J.: Lawrence Erlbaum.

References for studies exploring the relationship of attributions and dysfunctional behavior include: Martinko, M. J. & Gardner, W. L. 1982. Learned helplessness: An alternative explanation for performance deficits. *Academy of Management Review*, 7(2), 195-204; Douglas, S. C. & Martinko, M. J. 2001. Exploring the role of individual differences in the prediction of workplace aggression. *Journal of Applied Psychology*, 86(4), 547-559; Martinko, M. J. & Zellars, K. 1998. Toward a theory of workplace violence and aggression: A cognitive appraisal perspective. In Griffin, R. W., O'Leary-Kelly, A., & Collins, J. M. (Eds.). *Dysfunctional Behavior in Organizations: Violent and Deviant Behavior*, Stamford, CT: JAI Press, 1-42; and Martinko, M. J., Henry, J., and Zmud, R. 1996. Learned Helplessness: A theoretical explication of reactions to information technologies in the workplace. *Behavior and Information Technology*, 15(5), 313-330.

Discussions of self-efficacy and self-esteem occur in: Mossholder, K. & Bedian, A.G., & Armenakis, A.A. 1982. Group process-work outcome relationships: A note on the moderating effect of self-esteem. *Academy of Management Journal*, 271-288; Bandura, A. 1982. Self-efficacy mechanisms in human agency, *American Psychologist*, 37, 122-147; Stajkovic, A. D. & Luthans, F. 1998. Self-efficacy and work related performance: A meta-analysis. *Psychological Bulletin*, September, 240-261.

The classic reference for the work on emotional intelligence is: Goleman, D. 1995. *Emotional Intelligence*, New York: Bantam.

References for work in the area of impression management are as follows: Gardner, W. L. & Martinko, M. J. 1988. Impression Management in Organizations. *Journal of Management*, 14(2), 321-338; Gardner, W. L. & Martinko, M. J. 1988. Impression Management: An Observational Study Linking Audience Characteristics with Verbal Self-Presentations.

Academy of Management Journal, 31 (1), 42-65; Kilduff, M. & Day, D.V. 1994. Do chameleons get ahead? The effects of self-monitoring on managerial careers, *Academy of Management Journal*, 1047-1060.

The role of attributions in cross-cultural management is addressed in: Martinko, M. J. & Douglas, S. C. 1999. Culture and expatriate failure: An attributional explication. The *International Journal of Organizational Analysis*, 7(3), 266-294.

Some basic readings for charismatic and transformational leadership are: Conger, J.A. & Kanungo, R. 1987. Toward a behavioral theory of charismatic leadership in organizational settings. *Academy of Management Review*, 12, 637-647; Bass, B.M. 1990. From transactional to transformational leadership: Learning to share the vision, *Organizational Dynamics*, Winter, 19-31.

ABOUT THE AUTHOR

Mark J. Martinko was born in Cleveland, Ohio. He is the second of four brothers and has one sister. He attended Holy Name High School, graduated from Muskingum College with a B.S. degree in psychology in 1971, and received an M.A. degree with an emphasis in child psychology from the College of Education at the University of Iowa in 1973. He received his Ph.D. in Business from the University of Nebraska in 1977. After completing his doctoral work, he remained at the University of Nebraska for one year as a visiting assistant professor and then accepted a position at Florida State University in 1978 where he is now a professor of management and teaches at the undergraduate and graduate levels in the areas of organizational behavior, change, research methods, and leadership.

In the process of completing his education he worked a number of jobs including caddie, car mechanic, cook (McDonald's), retail sales, underground and overhead construction (Cleveland Electric Illuminating Company), carpet installer, steelworker (U.S. Steel), and has worked on assembly lines at Sheller-Globe Corporation and National Cash Register. After receiving his master's degree from the University of Iowa, he worked for Western Electric Corporation as a management trainer and then at Omaha Public Power District, also conducting management training. He has also served as a consultant and trainer for a wide variety of organizations including Wal-Mart Corporation; Omaha Public Power District; Guinness Group Sales, Ireland; Shell Oil; W. R. Grace Corporation; and the Florida Departments of Education, Transportation, Law Enforcement, Human Services, Insurance, and Labor. His most interesting consultancy was with Guinness Group Sales of Ireland where, over a period of five years, he conducted participant observation studies to assess the dynamics of stout and lager consumption as a basis for developing marketing strategies in Ireland.

Throughout his career, Mark's research has focused on leadership and motivation. He is the co-author of *The Power of Positive Reinforcement* and *The Practice of Supervision and Management* and recently edited *Attribution Theory: An Organizational Perspective* which has been cited as one of the two most influential books on management thought in 1995. He has contributed more than 50 research articles in respected academic journals including: *Academy of Management Review, Academy of Management Journal, Journal of Applied Psychology, Organizational Behavior and Human Decision Processes, Journal of Management Studies, Journal of Management, Journal of Organizational Behavior, American Educational Research Journal, Group and Organization Studies,* and the *Journal of Organizational Behavior Management*. He served two successive three-year terms on the editorial board of the *Academy of Management Review*. He currently serves on the editorial boards of the *Journal of Organizational Behavior Management* and *Organizational Dynamics*. He is a past president of the Southern Management Association and the Allied Southern Business Association.

Upon moving to Florida, Mark took Captain Cook's advice and married a native. His wife Elda is a territory manager for Pfizer Pharmaceuticals. Their son Daniel is an avid football and roller-hockey player and is beginning high school. Mark's recreational activities include golfing (13 handicap) and salt-water fishing. He and Daniel caught a 450 lb. blue marlin in 1999. He has caught numerous sailfish on a fly rod, beginning in 1994.

HOW TO ORDER

If this book is not available at your local bookstore, you can order it for $19.95 in paperback or $29.95 in hardback, plus $3.00 for shipping and handling, from Gulf Coast Publishing, 3779 Forsythe Way, Tallahassee, FL 32308, by calling 850-893-2786, or by email: martinko@netttally.com